PENGUIN  CLASSICS

THE SONG OF ROLAND

GLYN S. BURGESS studied French at St John's College, Oxford. He then took his MA at McMaster University, Hamilton, Ontario, and went on to do a doctorate at the Sorbonne. He has taught at Queen's University, Kingston, Ontario, at the University of South Carolina, and, since 1971, at the University of Liverpool, where he is currently Professor of French and Head of the Department. His interests lie in early medieval French literature, especially in the relationship between literature and society. In addition to the present volume, he has translated (with Keith Busby) the *Lais* of Marie de France for Penguin Classics, and he has published widely on twelfth-century courtly literature, especially on the *Lais* of Marie de France. His publications include *Contribution à l'étude du vocabulaire pré-courtois* (1977), *Marie de France: an Analytical Bibliography* (1977; first supplement 1986), *Chrétien de Troyes: Erec et Enide* (1984), *The Lais of Marie de France: Text and Context* (1987) and *The Old French Narrative Lay: an Analytical Bibliography* (1995). He has been associated since its inception in the mid 1970s with the International Courtly Literature Society, of which he was President from 1989 to 1995.

The Song of Roland

TRANSLATED WITH AN INTRODUCTION
AND NOTES BY

GLYN BURGESS

PENGUIN BOOKS

PENGUIN BOOKS

Published by the Penguin Group
Penguin Books Ltd, 80 Strand, London WC2R 0RL, England
Penguin Putnam Inc., 375 Hudson Street, New York, New York 10014, USA
Penguin Books Australia Ltd, 250 Camberwell Road, Camberwell, Victoria 3124, Australia
Penguin Books Canada Ltd, 10 Alcorn Avenue, Toronto, Ontario, Canada M4V 3B2
Penguin Books India (P) Ltd, 11 Community Centre, Panchsheel Park, New Delhi – 110 017, India
Penguin Books (NZ) Ltd, Cnr Rosedale and Airborne Roads, Albany, Auckland, New Zealand
Penguin Books (South Africa) (Pty) Ltd, 24 Sturdee Avenue, Rosebank 2196, South Africa

Penguin Books Ltd, Registered Offices: 80 Strand, London WC2R 0RL, England

www.penguin.com

This translation first published 1990
28

Copyright © Glyn Burgess, 1990
All rights reserved

Printed in England by Clays Ltd, St Ives plc
Filmset in Linotron Plantin

Except in the United States of America, this book is sold subject
to the condition that it shall not, by way of trade or otherwise, be lent,
re-sold, hired out, or otherwise circulated without the publisher's
prior consent in any form of binding or cover other than that in
which it is published and without a similar condition including this
condition being imposed on the subsequent purchaser

ISBN-13: 978–0–140–44532–9

Contents

Introduction

The Bodleian Library in Oxford houses a small, rather insignificant manuscript designated as Digby 23 and containing a poem which lacks a title. This poem was first published (Paris, 1837) under the title *La Chanson de Roland ou de Roncevaux* by Francisque Michel, who records how he discovered it in July 1835. It has come to be known simply as the *Chanson de Roland* (*Song of Roland*). The manuscript, executed in the twelfth century (probably between 1130 and 1170), presents a number of linguistic features reflecting the Anglo-Norman dialect, the French spoken in England for some three hundred years after the Norman Conquest. It contains a number of errors committed by the scribe and has been touched up in over sixty places by a twelfth-century reviser. Manuscript Digby 23 is certainly not the poet's original, but some of the errors suggest that it represents the copy of a copy of the original (see Whitehead, pp. vi–vii).* It is also not the only surviving manuscript of the *Song of Roland*. Two versions in the Library of St Mark in Venice (fourteenth century, known as Venice IV; late thirteenth century, known as Venice VII), versions in the Municipal Libraries of Châteauroux (late thirteenth century) and Lyon (fourteenth century), in the Bibliothèque Nationale in Paris (late thirteenth century), in Trinity College, Cambridge (fifteenth century) and some fragmentary French texts attest to the popularity of the legend of Roland, even when they lack the sophistication and poetic density of the Oxford text. These French versions are derived, like that in Digby 23, from a lost original (see Segre, p. xiv). Also extant are adaptations into Middle High German (the *Ruolandsliet*), Old Norse (the *Karlamagnus-*

---

* Full details of works referred to are given in the Bibliography, pp. 162–3.

INTRODUCTION

saga), Welsh (*Cân Rolant*), Dutch (the *Roelantslied*) and Middle English (*Song of Roland*).

The precise date of composition of the Oxford version is difficult to determine. The numerous proper names, of individuals and places, seem at first sight to offer a fruitful source of information. But many appear to be the product of poetic invention. Some, however, have made scholars wonder whether the poet had in mind a specific historical event. Allusions to the Col de Cize (vv. 583, 719, 2939), Tudela (v. 200) and Valterne (vv. 199, 931, 1291, interpreted as Valterra on the River Ebro) may be a reflection of battles fought in these places at the end of the eleventh century. The statement, placed in the mouth of a pagan, that Charles crossed the sea to England (v. 372) looks like a reference to William I and the Norman Conquest, and mention of victories in Apulia and Calabria could well reflect the activities of the Norman Robert Guiscard in southern Italy in the later years of the eleventh century. In his *Roman de Rou*, written about 1160, the poet Wace claims that a song of Roland was sung to the Normans by a certain Taillefer before the battle of Hastings.*

The poem has been dated as early as 1060 and as late as the second half of the twelfth century, but the most frequently accepted date is around the very end of the eleventh century (1098–1100). This would place the poem at the time of the First Crusade. Indeed the inclusion of a relic of the Holy Lance in Charlemagne's sword (vv. 2501–9) has been seen as an allusion to the revelation to Peter Bartholomew which resulted in the discovery of the Lance of the Crucifixion in Antioch in 1098. This discovery improved the morale of the Crusaders, who were under siege from the forces of Kerbogha, and they immediately used it in their successful battle in June 1098 against their Arab and Turkish opponents. The setting of the *Song of Roland* is northern Spain and Charles himself did lead a campaign in Spain in the eighth century. In the eleventh century Christian forces, consisting mainly of Franks, also undertook expeditions to Spain. But the overall spirit of the poem appears to be that of the First Crusade. All in all the

* *Le Roman de Rou de Wace*, ed. A. J. Holden, 3 vols (Paris, Picard, 1970–73), II, vv. 8013–18 (see also v. 8935).

8

various elements which have significance for the dating of the text, including linguistic features, do not seem opposed to a date just before or just after the Christians captured Jerusalem in 1099 (for further information see Le Gentil, pp. 22–31, English edition, pp. 16–24).

The story recounted in the *Song of Roland* has a certain historical foundation. The context is the dissension in the Muhammadan world which crept in around the year 750. Charles entered Spain in the year 778 at the solicitation of the governor of Barcelona, Suleiman ibn-al-Arabi, who sought his assistance against his enemy Abderrahman. Charles was promised in return the surrender of several cities in Spain. After a few months of campaigning and while he was besieging Saragossa, Charles was informed of a Saxon uprising in the north. He lifted the siege and began to make his way back to France, taking Suleiman with him as a prisoner. The latter's promises had not been adequately fulfilled and Charles probably suspected him of treachery. On the way back he destroyed Pamplona, to prevent it from rebelling against him, and drove out many of its inhabitants. As the Franks were crossing the Pyrenees on 15 August 778 their rearguard was ambushed by Basques. Their baggage train was pillaged and all the members of the rearguard were slaughtered. The ambush took place in the pass of Roncesvalles (Old French Rencesvals, French Roncevaux). This defeat taught Charles a lesson and his attitude towards Spain became defensive. He eventually managed, with the capture of Barcelona in 803, to establish as a buffer zone an area of Frankish influence known as the Spanish March. The best-known account of these happenings is preserved in the *Vita Karoli Magni* of Einhard, written some fifty or sixty years after the event. Einhard tells us that the loss of the rearguard was due to Basque/Gascon treachery and that this was the only loss sustained by Charlemagne during his energetic attacks against Spain:

At a moment when Charlemagne's army was stretched out in a long column of march, as the nature of the local defiles forced it to be, these Basques [Wascones], who had set their ambush on the very top of one of the mountains, came rushing down on the last part of the baggage train and the troops who were marching in support of the rearguard and so protecting the army which had gone on ahead. The Basques forced them down into the valley beneath, joined battle with them and killed them to the last man. They then snatched up the baggage, and, protected as they were by the cover of darkness, which was just beginning to fall, scattered in all directions without losing a moment. In this feat the Basques were helped by the lightness of their arms and by the nature of the terrain in which the battle was fought. On the other hand, the heavy nature of their own equipment and the unevenness of the ground completely hampered the Franks in their resistance to the Basques. In this battle died Eggihard, who was in charge of the King's table, Anshelm, the Count of the palace and Roland, Lord of the Breton Marches, along with a great number of others. What is more, this assault could not be avenged there and then, for, once it was over, the enemy dispersed in such a way that no one knew where or among which people they could be found.*

Particularly noticeable in this account is the presence of Roland and the absence of other protagonists of the *Song of Roland* such as Ganelon, Oliver or Archbishop Turpin. The stress laid by Einhard on the element of treachery is also of significance. The Franks may have considered that the Basques who attacked the rearguard were particularly at fault because they owed some form of allegiance to Charlemagne. For the author of the *Song of Roland*, writing over three hundred years after the event, the element of treachery offered dramatic possibilities which could be harnessed to a transformation in the identity of the opposition. In the poem itself the enemy becomes, not the Basques or the Gascons, but the Muslims, whom the poet calls Saracens. This change permits the clash to be raised to the status of a struggle between Christians and pagans. We can also note that in the poem Roland is presented as a Frank from France, not as a Breton.

The story as told by the poet of the *Song of Roland* is as follows. Charlemagne has been successfully campaigning in Spain for seven

---

* The quotation is taken from *Einhard and Notker the Stammerer, Two Lives of Charlemagne*, translated by L. Thorpe (Harmondsworth, Penguin Books, 1969), pp. 64–5. Thorpe dates the Einhard text between 829 and 836 (p. 2).

years. Only one obstacle remains, the city of Saragossa, which is held by a pagan, King Marsile. The pagans hold a council in which a plan is hatched. Blancandrin, whose plan it is, will go to Charlemagne's camp and request that he should return to his capital at Aix-la-Chapelle. Marsile will follow him there, become his vassal and embrace the Christian faith. Hostages will be offered to Charlemagne by way of security. The Franks summon a council to discuss this offer and Roland is the first to speak. He is adamantly opposed to the idea on the grounds of earlier treacherous behaviour on the part of the pagans. On a former occasion Charlemagne had sent two of his counts as messengers to Marsile and their heads had been removed. Roland reminds Charlemagne that it is his duty to avenge the death of his vassals. After a period of silence, Ganelon, Roland's stepfather, responds and claims that Roland's advice is not in the interests of the Franks. Such arrogant and foolish advice should not be heeded. Ganelon's view is supported by Duke Naimes, one of the wisest counsellors at the court. His reason for advising acceptance of Marsile's terms is that it would be wrong to continue to wage war against an enemy who is on the point of defeat and who asks for mercy. The Franks add their assent and there remains only the question of the appointment of an ambassador. Roland offers to go, as do Naimes, Oliver and Archbishop Turpin. Eventually it is Ganelon, nominated by Roland, who is appointed. Ganelon's extraordinarily aggressive reaction to his appointment hints at some unexplained enmity between them.

A crucial section of the text is the journey back to Marsile's camp during which Blancandrin exploits Ganelon's evident dislike of Roland. Ganelon in due course suggests to Marsile himself that, if he wants peace, he should aim to bring about the death of Roland, Charlemagne's right arm. Ganelon pledges to ensure that Roland is in the rearguard along with Oliver and their twenty thousand men. On Ganelon's return to Charles Roland is duly appointed as captain of the rearguard at Ganelon's instigation, in spite of the misgivings of Charles himself who launches an attack on Ganelon, whom he calls a 'living devil' (v. 746). The Franks set out for France and the pagans lie in wait. When the battle approaches, we see how well equipped and well organized the pagans are. To maximize the effect of their charge they make use of the bright light, the reflection of the sun on their shining armour and the noise of a thousand bugles. It is Oliver who first realizes that a battle is inevitable and when he makes the point to Roland, the latter responds: 'And may God grant it to us' (v. 1008). Roland's view is that it is a vassal's duty to fight for his lord. Moreover, he is determined that his reputation and that of his family will not suffer. The justification for the battle is that 'The pagans are wrong and the Christians are right' (v. 1015).

In a key passage Oliver asks Roland to blow his horn, the oliphant, in order to bring back the main body of the army. Roland refuses in the name of his own and his family's honour and states his intention to strike great blows with his sword Durendal. The early skirmishes go the way of the Franks. Roland begins the battle by dispatching Marsile's nephew and this is followed by victories for Oliver, who slays Marsile's brother, for Archbishop Turpin, who kills the Saracen king Corsablix, and for several members of the group known as the twelve Peers. But gradually the superior numbers of the pagans begin to tell. Roland reverses his earlier decision and blows his oliphant. Eventually Oliver dies, having been fatally wounded by Marsile's uncle. But the pagans, hearing the sound of Charles's trumpets, flee, leaving only Roland and Turpin on the field. Roland gathers up the bodies of his dead companions and arranges them before the archbishop who blesses them. Turpin finally dies while trying to fetch water for Roland, who has lost consciousness. Roland's own death, preceded by his attempt to prevent Durendal and the oliphant from falling into enemy hands, is the most dramatic moment in the poem.

Charlemagne arrives on the field of battle after Roland's death and is plunged into the bitterest grief. The daylight is extended for him by God and his pursuit of the Saracens ends when they are killed or drowned as they try to cross the River Ebro. Marsile manages to return to Saragossa. We now hear that Baligant, emir of Babylon and leader of all Islam, has belatedly responded to an earlier request for help by Marsile. Learning to his surprise that Marsile has been defeated and that Charles is close at hand, he prepares for battle. Charles, meanwhile, returns to the scene of the destruction of his rearguard, finds, to his great grief, the body of

Roland and prepares to bury the dead. He is interrupted by news of
the approach of Baligant's forces and the ensuing battle, preceded
by the lengthy marshalling of the Christian and pagan divisions,
rages throughout the entire day. It ends when Charlemagne him-
self kills Baligant, after a monumental single combat in which only
Saint Gabriel's assistance prevents Charles from succumbing to a
mighty blow from the emir. News of the defeat hastens Marsile's
death and Charles takes the city of Saragossa and holds Queen
Bramimonde prisoner. He quickly returns to France to prepare the
trial of Ganelon. His first task is to face Roland's fiancée Aude,
Oliver's sister, who, on discovering that Roland is dead, dies of a
broken heart.

The trial begins once the judges have arrived from the various
corners of Charlemagne's empire. Charles, as the plaintiff, puts the
case against Ganelon: for a gift of money Ganelon took from him
Roland, Oliver and the other members of the rearguard. Ganelon
accepts this, but refuses to consider it as treason. He sought
Roland's death because of some unspecified financial trickery on
Roland's part (v. 3758). He adds that Roland conceived a hatred of
him and nominated him for a deadly mission. As Roland had
received a challenge in due form, he was the victim of vengeance,
not treason. Thirty of Ganelon's relatives pledge their support for
him, amongst whom is the powerful figure of Pinabel. The judges
decide that Charles should be requested to let Ganelon off on this
occasion, so that he can continue to provide him with feudal
service. Nothing can bring Roland back. Charles castigates the
judges as traitors (*felun*, v. 3814) and only the intervention of
Thierry of Anjou saves the day for Charles. Thierry argues that,
when serving Charles, Roland should have been protected from this
sort of vengeance and that Ganelon is indeed a traitor who should
be hanged. A judicial combat ensues in which Thierry, although by
far the smaller man, defeats Pinabel thanks to the protection of
God. Ganelon's supporters are hanged and he himself is torn apart
by four horses. Bramimonde is baptized and christened Juliana.
Charles's tribulations are not at an end, as the archangel Gabriel an-
nounces to him that he must make his way to Imphe in order to help
a certain King Vivien who is under attack from pagans. Wearily
Charles foresees the continuation of his struggle against Islam.

There can be no certainties regarding the author of this poem. The final line (*'Ci falt la geste que Turoldus declinet'*, v. 4002) at least offers us a name, but whether Turoldus (Turold or Thorold) was the author of the entire Oxford version, of part of it, of its source, or whether he was just its copyist is a matter for conjecture. The meaning of the verb *decliner* here is in doubt: 'to relate, compose, complete, copy, recite, decline in health, approach one's end, etc.'. Jenkins thinks that 'Turold [its author or redactor] is becoming increasingly infirm' (p. 279, see also p. xlvi). My own preference is to see Turoldus as the author, relating his own version of a heroic poem which would have existed in a variety of earlier states. He was clearly an exceptionally learned and gifted man, a member of the lower or the higher clergy. There are frequent references to Biblical incidents and the practices of the Church. He was also a man well versed in military matters, one capable of composing a poem with the capacity to inspire feudal lords with crusading zeal. Tantalizingly there are several Turolduses or Thorolds who go some way towards fitting this description. There was a Thorold who was the son or nephew of William the Conqueror's half-brother, Odo, Bishop of Bayeux. After the battle of Hastings William made him Abbot of Malmesbury and he later became Abbot of Burton-on-Trent and then in 1069 of Peterborough. This Thorold died in 1098. Even more promising is Thorold of Envermeu who succeeded Odo as Bishop of Bayeux in 1097. He was chaplain to William Rufus after his capture of Normandy in 1090 and earlier usher to Robert, Duke of Normandy. After seven years as bishop he was deposed by Pope Paschal II and withdrew to the monastery of Bec. The political nature of his appointment as bishop and his experience as a courtier provide him with suitable credentials. He could have completed his poem at Bec, which had close relations with the monastery of Mont St Michel, referred to in v. 1428, perhaps from some personal knowledge, as Seint Michel del Peril because of its dangerous situation on the sea (*in periculo maris*).

The *Song of Roland* is almost certainly the oldest extant epic poem in French. Such poems are also called *chansons de geste*. The Latin term *gesta* means 'things which have been done, deeds, actions', and the Old French term *geste* has a similar meaning, with particular application to heroic deeds. *Chanter de geste* is 'to sing an epic song'. But the term *geste* in Old French can also cover the notions of 'family', 'people', 'race' or 'history' and refer to an account of the deeds of a nation or a kinship group. As the present poem reveals (vv. 788, 1443, 1685, 2095, 3181, 3262, 3742), these meanings can to a certain extent overlap and in the final line of the poem ('*Ci falt la geste que Turoldus declinet*') the sense is perhaps no more than 'story, account'. In the early thirteenth century, the epic poems in French, which had become exceedingly popular during the twelfth century, were grouped by scribes into *gestes* or cycles. The *Song of Roland* belongs to the Cycle of the King (*Geste du roi*), a category which includes the *Pilgrimage of Charlemagne* (*Le Pèlerinage de Charlemagne* or *Le Voyage de Charlemagne*), which at times seems to be a parody of the *Roland*. The other two principal cycles were the Feudal Cycle (*Geste de Doon de Maiance*) and the William Cycle (*Geste de Guillaume d'Orange* or *Geste de Garin de Monglane*). In all there are around a hundred surviving *chansons de geste* dating from around 1100 to the second half of the fourteenth century.

A *chanson de geste* is presented in the form of units or verse paragraphs called *laisses* which are of different length. Some of these *laisses* can be as short as three or four lines and others contain well over a hundred lines. The average length for the *Roland* is under fourteen lines. In some cases it is not easy to know where a new *laisse* begins. The manuscript of the *Song of Roland* has 291 *laisses*, but editors vary in their treatment of the *laisse* divisions. For example, Whitehead, on whose edition this translation is largely based, has 298 *laisses*, whereas Jenkins has 290. The rhyming scheme of the *chansons* is either assonance, in which only the final stressed vowels are identical throughout the *laisse*, or rhyme, in which both the final consonants and the final stressed vowels are identical. In the *Roland* the *laisses* are assonanced, but one poem from the Feudal Cycle, *Raoul de Cambrai* (composed around 1180), contains two parts, the first in rhyme, the second in assonance. The length of the entire poems varies from the 870 lines of the *Pilgrimage of Charlemagne* to over 30,000 lines. The number of syllables per line is normally ten, with a caesura after the fourth syllable. This is the case with the *Song of Roland* (but around 320 lines are irregular). The twelve-syllable line, the alexandrine, is used by the author of the *Pilgrimage*, composed around the middle of the twelfth century, but in general this metre is more characteristic of the later epics. There is one early epic, *Gormont et Isembart*, extant only in a six-hundred-line fragment, which makes use of an eight-syllable line. In the later medieval period some of the best-known verse epics were put into prose and they remained popular in this form until the nineteenth century.

The *Song of Roland*, as it appears in the Digby 23 manuscript, contains 3998 largely decasyllabic verses, which editors, assuming a few blank lines, expand to 4002 verses. It will have been performed by a *jongleur* to the accompaniment of a stringed instrument called the *vielle* (Modern English 'viol'). The *jongleur* (Old French *jogler*, *jogleor*) was an itinerant minstrel who provided his audience with a wide variety of entertainment, one aspect of which has survived in the English term juggler. We have virtually no knowledge of the music which accompanied the *chanson de geste*. It was probably a simple, monotonous tune repeated unchanged line after line. The mysterious letters AOI, which occur after many of the *laisses* and occasionally within a *laisse*, may have had something to do with the musical presentation. But amongst other explanations for these letters, which are not found elsewhere, are that they indicate some form of special emphasis; the introduction of a change of scene, action or speaker; a war-cry uttered by the performer or the audience; or a note made by the scribe relating to the process of copying. The presentation of any *chanson de geste* by the *jongleur* would certainly have been an artistic performance and the various minstrels would have been able to use their personal skills in the areas of drama and musicianship in order to please their public. We can assume that *jongleurs*, equipped with a stock of *chansons de geste* and works in other genres, would have been capable of all forms of improvisation. Performing wherever a sufficient number of people had gathered together, at a fair, a marriage celebration, after dinner in a castle, they may only have had time for a few key passages from the *Roland* or other poems and had to set the scene by summarizing earlier events.

Of all the extant *chansons de geste* the *Roland* has the most exceptional poetic and dramatic qualities, as a close reading reveals. Amongst the stylistic aspects which become immediately apparent are the paratactic structure, the use of tenses and the presence of formulas. Parataxis is the placing of clauses in a sentence side by side, without the connection between them being specifically stated. If we take, for example, the opening lines of *laisse* 27, when Ganelon is preparing to act as messenger to King Marsile, we get the following results. The first line (v. 342) tells us that Ganelon goes to his lodging (*'Guenes li quens s'en vait a sun ostel'*). The next line informs us that he begins to arm himself (*'De guarnemenz se prent a cunreer'*). The two actions each take up a whole line and they are clearly related. But no conjunction or adverb is provided ('and', 'then', 'immediately', 'later', etc.). In the third line the nature of the armour is described, the best he could lay hands on (*'De ses meillors que il pout recuvrer'*). This line would not stand alone, and it contains within it a relative clause ('which he could . . .'). There is a link here to the preceding line, but through the preposition *de*, not a conjunction or adverb. The next four lines are again simply single line statements: he fastened his spurs on his feet (*'Esperuns d'or ad en ses piez fermez'*), he girded on his sword (*'Ceint Murglies s'espee a sun costéd'*), he mounted his horse (*'En Tachebrun, sun destrer, est muntéd'*), his uncle held his stirrup (*'L'estreu li tint sun uncle Guinemer'*). These seven lines present evident difficulties both of translation and of punctuation (my punctuation differs significantly from that of F. Whitehead). It is not certain whether some of the statements made by the poet are juxtaposed clauses within a sentence or sentences in their own right.

The seven lines in this passage also illustrate the complexities of tense usage in the *Song of Roland*. The author begins with two present tenses (*vait*, *prent*) and then moves to a preterite in the relative clause (*pout*). He follows this with a present perfect (*ad fermez*), returns to the present (*ceint*), goes back to the present perfect (*est muntéd*) and then produces another preterite (*tint*). The present and preterite tenses offer no problems of translation other than the fact that the combined effect is surprising to the modern reader. It is tempting to keep all these tenses in the present or, more likely, to tell the entire story in the past tense: 'Ganelon went to his lodgings, armed himself and put on his spurs . . .' The present perfects are more difficult. When we read in v. 345 that literally

'Spurs of gold has [Ganelon] on his feet fixed', we have to be aware that in Old French the form *fermez* 'fixed' was an adjective and not just a past participle, as in Modern French. He has them on his feet in a state of having been fixed. The next line but one tells us that he is in a state of having mounted his horse (*est muntéd*). There is no adequate way of translating these present perfects into English. It does seem possible to say 'Spurs of gold are fixed to his feet', but this does not make it clear who did the fixing. For *est muntéd* I have fallen back on the use of the English past tense, 'he mounted', which is preferable to the present perfect tense 'he has mounted'. Once the lack of conjunctions, which creates difficulty in understanding the relationship between the author's single-line statements, is coupled with the frequent shift in tenses, we begin to envisage some of the subtleties of the poem. What precisely is the causal, temporal and sequential link between the events and the ideas expressed?

This problem takes on a new twist in the parallel *laisses* which the author introduces from time to time. In *laisse* 80 Oliver is on the top of a hill from where he sees the approach of the pagan forces. He reports his findings to Roland and accuses Ganelon of treachery. In *laisse* 81 he is back at the top of the hill, still studying the pagan forces. This time the poet gives more details about them and about Oliver's reaction. This is followed apparently by three requests by Oliver to Roland that he should blow his horn. There are three refusals made in similar, but not identical terms (*laisses* 83–5). Later Roland's death is described in three *laisses* (174–6). He appears to offer his right glove to God on three occasions (vv. 2365, 2373, 2389). What is actually happening here? Does Oliver come down the hill and go back up? Is Roland's glove presented three times or just once? By breaking the temporal sequence and slowing down the narration of events at a particularly sensitive moment the poet can add to the drama of the account and intensify its poetic potential.

Poetic intensity can also be created or enhanced by the use of formulas. The first of the three *laisses* relating Roland's death opens with the phrase '*Ço sent Rollant*', 'Roland feels' (v. 2355). So does the second (v. 2366). This state of affairs has been prepared by the use of the same formula at the beginning of *laisses* 168, 170 and 171.

When Oliver in *laisse* 80 climbs his hill only to discover the approach of the Saracens, we read: '*Oliver est desur un pui halçur*' ('Oliver is on a lofty hilltop'). The following *laisse* begins: '*Oliver est desur un pui muntét*' ('Oliver has climbed a hill'). The next two *laisses* begin with the phrase '*Dist Oliver*', 'Oliver said' (vv. 1039, 1049) and the following two with '*Cumpainz Rollant*' (vv. 1059, 1070). Roland's three replies to Oliver contain various formulas which are very skilfully varied. Roland condemns the pagans to disaster in v. 1057 ('*Felun paien mar i vindrent as porz*') and again in v. 1068 ('*Felun paien mar i sunt asemblez*'). The variation in formulas helps to alleviate the somewhat monotonous nature of Roland's replies.

The *Song of Roland* without doubt owes a great deal to oral composition and the use of formulas is entirely natural. There has been a good deal of discussion in recent years about the precise definition of the formula, about its use by various poets and about what formulaic expressions tell us concerning the methods of composition of the authors. Formulas have been used to show which poems are orally composed and which written compositions. They are phrases which can admit of slight variations but which fulfil a specific semantic, metrical and syntactical function. They can occupy the first half of a line (the first hemistich) or the second half (the second hemistich). In the hands of a great poet they can, whether or not they are drawn from a general stockpile of such phrases, be used to create an original poem. It has been said that for the epic the entire poem is formulaic, but perhaps the densest and most obvious use of formulas in the *Song of Roland* occurs in the battle scenes (see Appendix vv. 1188–268). Here phrases such as '*Sun cheval brochet*', 'He spurs on his horse' (v. 1197), '*Vait le ferir*', 'He goes to strike him' (v. 1198) and '*L'escut li frient*', 'He breaks his shield' (v. 1199) are repeated several times as the various pagans are dealt with by the Franks. The fact that the second hemistichs are varied adds to the interest of the poem and, as in the case of the quarrel between Oliver and Roland, prevents potential monotony.

The poet of the *Roland* uses his decasyllabic line, his *laisses* and his various stylistic techniques to narrate events which took place over three hundred years earlier. The principal protagonists are the pagan forces under King Marsile, Saracen King of Spain, and the

Christian forces under the Emperor Charlemagne (Charles did not in fact become emperor until AD 800, twenty-two years after the battle). Charles was around thirty-six years old at the time of the battle and not over two hundred, as the Saracens allege (v. 524, etc.) The Christians are referred to both as Franks (*'Francs s'en irunt en France, la lur tere'*, v. 50) and the French (*'L'ost des Franceis verrez sempres desfere'*, v. 49). Since the poet normally uses the two designations interchangeably and as Charles was King of the Franks, I have chosen to retain Franks in this translation in preference to French which would be more appropriate for the poet's own times. In the second half of the poem there is some differentiation between groups within the Frankish empire, with references to such peoples as the Bretons (vv. 3052, 3702, 3961), the Normans (vv. 3045, 3470, 3702, etc.) and the Poitevins (vv. 3062, 3702, 3794, etc.). Just before he dies Roland makes it clear that he was the one who conquered for Charles a whole variety of territories, including Anjou, Brittany, Poitou, Maine, Normandy, Flanders and Burgundy (vv. 2322–34). The participants summoned for the trial of Ganelon (vv. 3700–3703, 3793–6), all of whom seem to be designated as Franks (vv. 3761, 3779), constitute a veritable roll-call of the Frankish empire. In addition to a variety of inhabitants of modern France, we find Bavarians, Saxons, Teutons and Germans.

After *laisse* 189 Charles has a second adversary in Baligant, emir of Babylon (Old Cairo). The exact status of the Baligant episode in relation to the poem has puzzled commentators. It can be regarded as unnecessary, once Marsile's forces have been dispatched into the River Ebro, as somewhat tedious in places, and generally as lacking the aesthetic qualities of much of the rest of the poem. But we have to admit that this episode is there in the Oxford version, even if it was added by a less talented poet. It has been argued that the addition of the Baligant episode is the major contribution of Turoldus himself. It has the advantage of raising the struggle between Charles and Marsile into one between Christianity and the fully-fledged might of paganism. Baligant brings with him a dazzling array of supporting troops: men from Butentrot, Milceni, Nubles, Blos, Bruns, Slavs, Sorbres, Sors, Armenians, Moors, men from Jericho, Nigres, Gros, Canaanites, Turks, Persians,

Petchenegs, Soltras, Avars, Ormaleus, Eugies, Samuel's people, men from Bruise, Clavers, etc. The Old French terms test the ingenuity of scholars in identifying the various peoples concerned, but they also attest to the great love of exotic names manifested by the poet of the Baligant episode and in fact of the whole text. We find nearly seventy Saracens mentioned by name in the text and the author clearly has a predilection for telling us that their home lies within a valley (Val Ferree, Val Fuit, Valfunde, Val Marchis, Val Metas, etc.), a location presumably deemed to be in keeping with their association with the devil. One of the pagans, Chernubles of Munigre, whose hair sweeps down to the ground, actually comes from the reputed home of the devils (v. 983). This is a place where the sun never shines, wheat cannot grow, rain never falls, no dew forms and where all the stones are black (vv. 975–82).

On the Frankish side the Twelve Peers play an important part. They are: Anscis, Berenger, Engeler, Gerin, Gerer, Gerard of Roussillon, Oliver, Oton, Roland, Samson, Yvon and Yvoire. The list of the Peers, who constitute Charles's chief warriors, varies from epic to epic and in the *Pilgrimage of Charlemagne* Duke Naimes and Archbishop Turpin are included amongst them (vv. 62–4). Roland, Charles's nephew, is without doubt the dominant figure. He is mentioned by name 187 times in the text. The first reference to him occurs in v. 104 and he is the first to respond when Charles asks the Franks for advice concerning Marsile's offer of peace (vv. 196–213). He is able to provide his companions with an impressive catalogue of his military achievements and subsequent events prove that he was right to reject Marsile's offer and to counsel continuing with the war. He offers to become Charles's messenger to Marsile (v. 254) and then, less satisfactorily, nominates his stepfather Ganelon for this appointment. There are clearly long-standing tensions between Roland and Ganelon and the quarrel which surfaces in the early Frankish council scenes constitutes another major conflict to add to that between the Saracens and the Franks. He antagonizes his stepfather by laughing at him (vv. 302–5) and the threat he poses to the Saracens is the major talking point on the journey from Charles's camp to that of Marsile (vv. 366–413).

When he knows that a battle must be fought against the

Saracens, Roland welcomes the opportunity this affords for demonstrating his commitment to feudal principles (vv. 1008–16). His determination to strike great blows with his sword, Durendal, and to avoid all forms of shame, for his country, his family and himself, are recurrent themes of the observations he makes to Oliver and explain his refusal to sound his horn. It is Roland who dispatches the first pagan, appropriately his opposite number, King Marsile's nephew, Aelroth (vv. 1188–212), and who, in his capacity as Charlemagne's right-hand man (v. 1195), removes the right hand of King Marsile (vv. 1903, 2701). Roland's lament for his dead companions (see Appendix, vv. 1851–85) is the one of the most poignant episodes in the battle and his ability to slice his victims down the middle in quick succession (e.g. vv. 1871–2) is quite awesome. In Archbishop Turpin's eyes he epitomizes the values of the true knight (vv. 1876–82). Roland's death, recounted at some length (vv. 2259–396) is central to the structure of the poem. He is killed by his effort in blowing his horn, late in the battle, an act which ruptures his temples. He is the only member of the rearguard not slain by a Saracen attack and it is his soul which is taken to Heaven by Saint Gabriel (v. 2395–6). His name and memory continue to dominate the Frankish reprisals and the scene in which Ganelon is tried for treason.

Oliver is the son of Duke Renier (v. 2208) and the brother of Roland's fiancée Aude. He is introduced in the same line as Roland (v. 104) and is constantly referred to as his companion. In conversation with Roland he stimulates important responses from him and is frequently the object of positive adjectives through which the poet stresses his worth, bravery, nobility and wisdom. His first action in the poem is to object to Roland's possible appointment as ambassador to Marsile and to offer to undertake this mission himself (vv. 255–8). He is the first to spot the advance of the pagans and to organize the Frankish troops for battle (v. 1046). He is immediately convinced that Roland should blow his horn and seek reinforcements (vv. 1050–92), but after Roland's refusal he enters the fray with vigour and dispatches Marsile's brother, Falsaron, the second pagan to attack (vv. 1213–34). His attempt to fight with a broken lance, which at Roland's insistence he eventually replaces with his sword Halteclere (vv. 1351–77), his opposition to Roland's

eventual decision to blow his horn (vv. 1702–11) and his attack on
Roland for displaying *estultie* and *legerie* instead of maintaining
vasselage and *mesure* (vv. 1723–6, all terms which are difficult to
define) add greatly to the dramatic structure of the poem. Oliver,
the brave and the courtly, is the only Frank, other than his nephew
Roland, to be mentioned by Charles on the occasion of his state-
ment of Ganelon's misdeeds (v. 3755).

Unlike Roland and Oliver, Charles is present in the poem from
the first *laisse* to the last. It has been suggested that the poem should
be called *The Song of Charlemagne* or at least the *The Song of Roland
and Charlemagne*. He attempts to do the right thing and to act
according to the wishes of his men (v. 167), but he is curiously weak
at times and ends up treating with the treacherous pagan king and
finally almost losing his case against Ganelon. His appearance and
his emotional reactions to events are leitmotifs of the poem: joy
(v. 96), anger (vv. 271, 1834), grief (vv. 830, 2880, 2936), tears
(vv. 841, 2856, 2873, 3725, 4001), the way he holds his head or tugs
at his beard (vv. 138–9, 2414, 3816), his fierce countenance (vv.
118, 142), his white beard and hoary-white hair (vv. 117, 261, 538,
4001). Einhard tells us what strong emotions the real Charlemagne
displayed (pp. 74–5). The last comment of the poem is placed in
Charlemagne's mouth: 'God, how wearisome my life is!' ('"*Deus*",
dist li reis, "*si penuse est ma vie!*"', v. 4000) and the poet's last
comment is to tell us of Charlemagne's tears and his act of pulling at
his beard ('*Pluret des oilz, sa barbe blanche tiret*', v. 4001).

The contribution made to the structure of the poem by other
Franks would be worthy of extended comment: Turpin, Naimes,
Thierry, perhaps Gautier del Hum. But one cannot conclude
without mentioning Ganelon. Like Charlemagne he is present
from the beginning of the poem to the end. He is said to have had a
prototype in Wanilo, who became Archbishop of Sens in 837 and
later, in 859, betrayed the cause of his benefactor Charles the Bald
(see Bédier, *Commentaires*, p. 513). Ganelon is first mentioned in
v. 178 and his blood pours forth on to the green grass of a meadow
near Aix in v. 3972. Introduced as the man who committed the act
of treason ('*ki la traïsun fist*', v. 178) he meets his end as an outright
traitor ('*fel recreant*', v. 3973). But the portrait we are given of him
is not entirely unfavourable. In the first Frankish council scene he

cuts a dashing figure with his marten skins, his silk tunic, his sparkling eyes, his fierce countenance and his impressively handsome physique (vv. 281–5). When he defends himself in his trial at Aix, he possesses a noticeably robust body and noble colouring ('*Cors ad gaillard, el vis gente color*', v. 3763), even after the battering he has received from Charles's servants (vv. 1823–7, 3737–9). His followers comment that he is a man of great nobility (v. 356) who has given his brother-in-law Charlemagne extended service (v. 351), a man who has always enjoyed an excellent reputation at court (v. 352). The poet stresses Ganelon's intelligence (*saveir*, vv. 369, 426) and he himself speaks with pride of the skilful way he extricated himself from the pagan camp ('*Par mun saveir vinc jo a guarisun*', v. 3774). But he does make the crucial speech objecting to Roland's demand that Charles should reject Marsile's offer of peace (vv. 220–29). He does negotiate a lucrative deal with Marsile (vv. 845–7) in which he also stands to achieve his ambition of ridding himself of that thorn in his flesh, his stepson Roland. Perhaps what the poet had in mind was that Ganelon was the devil in disguise, a man of outstanding appearance and abilities flawed by the presence within him of antisocial urges.

All these men are members of a feudal society. They are bound to each other by ties of fealty and homage. In a hierarchical system Charles is the lord of all the Franks and they are his vassals. They are committed to him, like any vassal to his lord, in honour and in all their goods ('*par honur e par ben*', v. 39), in love and faith ('*par amur e par feid*', vv. 86, 3801, 3810). They must endure any necessary form of suffering for their lord (vv. 1010–12, 1117–19) and they must not fail him (vv. 397, 1048). They must give him good advice (vv. 205–6, 228) and in general serve him to the best of their abilities, letting their courage (*vasselage*) bear witness to their commitment and enthusiasm. Oliver remarks poignantly to Roland that with the destruction of the rearguard Charles will never again receive their service ('*Jamais Karlon de nus n'avrat servise*', v. 1727). In return for his vassals' service a lord must protect them (v. 1864) and avenge them (vv. 213, 1459, 3975). Charles's senior vassals all have their own vassals, their own men. They become vassals with their hands joined together with those of their lord ('With his hands clasped in yours he will become your vassal', '*Qu'il devendrat jointes ses mains tis hom*', v. 223) and we can notice that this is the manner in which Roland passes away ('With his hands joined he went to his end', '*Juntes ses mains est alét a sa fin*', v. 2392).

The text is permeated by feudal terminology, feudal gestures, feudal attitudes. The men, Franks and Saracens, whose decisions carry weight, are counts, dukes and marquises. A general term for them is 'barons', the kings' senior counsellors. They are brave men who set great store by two things in particular: land and honour. They 'hold' their land from their lord (vv. 224, 2334) who gives it to them as a fief (v. 472, 2680), as a material reward for their service, to repay and secure their loyalty. Land becomes a form of tangible reality for them, an emotive concept. Blancandrin will sacrifice his own son in order that the Saracens will not lose their control over Spain (vv. 43–6, 57–9). The Franks fight for '*dulce France*', the fair land of France (twenty-three examples, vv. 16, 109, 116, 360, etc.). Fighting for their king, their lords, their faith, the Christians and the pagans actualize their values through violence, through the spilling of blood, through the power invested in their right arms and in their swords. The poet has his own ideals which he actualizes through the power of words, through his conviction of who is right and who is wrong, through his determination not to belie the *geste* of others who guarantee the accuracy of his information ('So says the annals [*geste*] and the man who was on the field', v. 2095; 'It is written in the ancient chronicle [*geste*]', v. 3742). At the close of the text the author sees the act of tearing Ganelon apart as a victory for vengeance and for justice, concepts which he appears to equate (vv. 3975, 3988). Moreover, the baptism of Bramimonde is presented as a victory for 'love' (v. 3674) and for 'truth' ('*veire conoisance*', v. 3987). In her conviction of the truth of Christianity, feudal, Christian and poetic values are united. Charlemagne has achieved an actual and a symbolic victory over paganism. Turoldus for his part has created his own new and authentic *geste*.

A Note on the Translation

My aim has been to translate the *Song of Roland* into straightforward modern English, rendering each line of text by one line of translation. No attempt has been made to reproduce the poetic qualities of the text other than through the act of rearranging the elements within each line, where necessary, to produce the most satisfactory rhythm in English. The paratactic structure of the Old French text (many of its lines are single entities without any clear link with the preceding or following line) can lead to a feeling of awkwardness in the English. Similarly the fact that Old French possesses two terms for the word 'and', *si* and *e(t)*, occasionally presents problems. I have, therefore, felt obliged from time to time, to sacrifice absolute fidelity to the detail of the text in order to achieve a more readable translation. The tenses of the original have, on the other hand, been maintained. This can produce slightly disconcerting shifts of tense in the English, but it has the advantage of presenting the time sequences in the way envisaged by the poet.

The reader will find in the Appendix a certain amount of the Old French text. The aim in editing these lines has been to reproduce those sections of the poem which are of particular significance for its meaning and structure. The lines of the text which are not found here have been translated from the edition by F. Whitehead (Oxford, Blackwell's French Texts, 2nd ed., 1946).

The Song of Roland

1

Charles the king, our great emperor,
Has been in Spain for seven long years,
And conquered that proud land as far as the sea.
There is no castle which can resist him,
No wall or city left to be destroyed,   5
Except for Saragossa, which stands upon a mountain.
It is held by King Marsile, who does not love God;
He serves Muhammad and calls upon Apollo.
He cannot prevent disaster from overtaking him.   AOI.

2

King Marsile was in Saragossa;   10
He went into a garden, beneath the shade,
And reclines upon a slab of bluish marble
With more than twenty thousand men around him.
He summons both his dukes and his counts:
'Hear, lords, what misfortune weighs upon us;   15
The emperor Charles from the fair land of France
Has come to this country to destroy us.
I have no army to match his in battle,
Nor sufficient men to break his army down.
Give me counsel as my wise men,   20
And protect me from both death and shame.'
There is no pagan who utters a single word in reply,
Except for Blancandrin from Castel de Valfunde.

3

Blancandrin was one of the wisest of the pagans,
25 A most valiant and worthy knight.
He was a man of great worth, helpful to his lord,
And he said to the king: 'Now do not be dismayed;
Offer Charles, the arrogant and cruel,
Faithful service and very great friendship.
30 Promise him bears and lions and dogs,
Seven hundred camels and a thousand moulted hawks,
Four hundred mules laden with gold and silver,
Fifty carts to carry it all away.
With this he will be able to pay his mercenaries well;
35 He has waged war long enough in this land,
The time is ripe for his return to Aix in France.
Tell him you will follow him there at Michaelmas
And receive the Christian faith;
You will be his vassal in honour and in all your goods.
40 If he asks for hostages, send him some,
Either ten or twenty, as a mark of good faith.
Let us send him the sons of our wives;
Even if it means his death, I shall send him mine.
Far better for them to lose their heads there
45 Than for us to lose our honour and our jurisdiction*
And be reduced to begging.'   AOI.

4

Blancandrin said: 'By this right hand of mine,
And by the beard which flutters against my chest,
You will soon see the Frankish host disband.
50 The Franks will return to France, their land;
When each man is in his own domain,
Charles will be in Aix, in his chapel;
At Michaelmas he will hold a great festival.
The day will arrive and the allotted time will pass;
55 He will hear no word or news from us.
The king is cruel, his temperament fierce;
He will have our hostages beheaded.

Far better for them to lose their heads there
Then for us to lose the fair and beautiful land of Spain
Or suffer misfortunes and privations.'   60
The pagans say: 'There is truth in this.'

5

King Marsile had finished his council
And he called Clarin of Balaguer,
Estamarin and Eudropin his peer
And Priamon and Guarlan the bearded,   65
Machiner and his uncle Matthew
And Jouner and Malbien of Outremer
And Blancandrin to serve as spokesman.
He summoned ten of his most treacherous men:
'Lord barons, you will go to Charlemagne;   70
He is besieging the city of Cordoba.
You will bear olive branches in your hands,
Signifying peace and humility.
If, by your skill, you can bring me peace,
I shall give you gold and silver in abundance,   75
Lands and fiefs, as many as you desire.'
The pagans say: 'This is a generous offer.'   AOI.

6

King Marsile had finished his council.
He said to his men: 'Lords, go now;
You will bear olive branches in your hands   80
And on my behalf speak to King Charlemagne,
Asking him, by his God, to have mercy on me.
He will not see the end of this first month
Without my following him with a thousand vassals.
I shall receive the Christian faith   85
And become his vassal in love and faith;
If he asks for hostages, he will receive some.'
Blancandrin said: 'You will have an excellent pact.' AOI.

7

Marsile had ten white mules brought forward
90 Which had been given to him by the King of Suatilie;
The bridles are of gold, the saddles trimmed with silver.
Those who carried the message mounted on their horses,
Bearing olive branches in their hands.
They came to Charles who holds France in his power;
95 There is nothing he can do to avoid deceit.   AOI.

8

The emperor is happy and joyful;
He has taken Cordoba and shattered its walls,
And demolished its towers with his catapults;
His knights have captured great booty,
100 Gold, silver and costly arms.
No pagan was left within the city
Who had not been slain or made a Christian.
The emperor is in a spacious garden;
With him are Roland and Oliver,
105 Samson the Duke and Anseis the fierce,
Geoffrey of Anjou, the king's standard bearer,
And Gerin and Gerer were there too.
Many others were with them;
There are fifteen thousand from the fair land of France.
110 The knights are seated on white silk brocade,
Amusing themselves by playing backgammon
And the wiser and older men play chess,
Whilst the agile young warriors practise fencing.
Beneath a pine tree, beside a wild briar bush,
115 There stands a chair of state, made from pure gold;
There sits the king who holds the fair land of France.
His beard is white and his hair hoary,
His stature is noble, his countenance fierce;
If anyone seeks him, there is no need to point him out.
120 The messengers got down from their horses
And greeted him with love and good will.

9

Blancandrin was the first to speak,
Saying to the king: 'May God protect you,
The Glorious One we must all adore.
King Marsile the valiant sends you this message: 125
He has long sought the faith which brings salvation
And wishes to give you a large portion of his wealth,
Bears and lions and chained hounds,
Seven hundred camels and a thousand moulted hawks,
Four hundred mules laden with gold and silver,   130
Fifty carts for you to carry it all away.
You will have enough gold bezants
To pay your mercenaries well.
You have been in this country a long time;
You should return to Aix in France.   135
There, my lord says, he will follow you.'
The emperor stretches out his hands towards God;
He lowers his head and begins to think.   AOI.

10

The emperor kept his head bowed;
He was not a man for hasty words.   140
His habit is to speak at leisure;
When he looks up, his countenance was fierce.
He said to the messengers: 'You have spoken well;
King Marsile is my sworn enemy:
In these words you have spoken here   145
To what extent can I place my confidence?'
'He offers you hostages,' said the Saracen,
'You will have ten or fifteen or twenty.
Even if it means his death, I shall send a son of mine,
And you will not have, I think, a nobler boy.   150
When you are in your royal palace,
At the great festival of Saint Michael of the Peril,
My Lord says he will follow you there.
In your baths, which God made for you there,
It is his wish to become a Christian.'   155
Charles replies: 'He may yet be saved.'   AOI.

11

The evening was fair and the sun was bright;
Charles has the ten mules stabled.
In the spacious garden the king has a tent pitched
160 And in it he lodged the ten messengers;
Twelve servants attended to all their needs.
They remain that night until the break of day;
The emperor arose early in the morning
And heard mass and matins.
165 Then the king went over to a pine tree;
He summons his barons to conclude his council.
He wishes to be guided entirely by the men of France.　　　AOI.

12

The emperor goes over to a pine tree;
He summons his barons to conclude his council,
170 Duke Ogier and Archbishop Turpin,
Richard the Old and his nephew Henry,
And the valiant Count Acelin of Gascony,
Tedbald of Reims and his cousin Milon,
And Gerer and Gerin were there too,
175 Along with them came Count Roland
And Oliver, the valiant and the noble.
There are more than a thousand Franks from France;
Ganelon came, who committed the act of treason.
Now begins the council which turned to grief.　　　AOI.

13

180 'My lord barons,' said the emperor Charles,
'King Marsile has sent me his messengers.
He wishes to give me a great portion of his wealth,
Bears and lions and trained hounds,
Seven hundred camels and a thousand moulted hawks,
185 Four hundred mules laden with Arabian gold,
And besides this more than fifty carts.
But he tells me I should return to France;

34

He will follow me to Aix, my home,
Where he will receive our most holy faith.
He will become a Christian, and hold his lands from me;   190
But I do not know what his true thoughts are.'
The Franks say: 'We must be on our guard.'   AOI.

14

The emperor had finished speaking.
Count Roland, who is not in agreement,
Rises to his feet, and spoke against the pact.   195
He said to the king: 'Believe Marsile and you will regret it.
We came to Spain seven long years ago;
I have conquered for you Noples and Commibles
And taken Valterne and the land of Pine,
And Balaguer, Tudela and Sezile.   200
King Marsile committed a most treacherous act;
He sent fifteen of his pagans,
Each bearing an olive branch.
They addressed you with these very same words;
You sought advice from your Franks   205
And they counselled you in somewhat reckless fashion.
You sent two of your counts to the pagans,
One was Basan, the other Basile.
He took their heads on the hills beneath Haltile.
Wage war, as you set out to do,   210
Take your assembled troops to Saragossa;
Lay siege to the city as long as you live,
And avenge those whom the traitor put to death.'   AOI.

15

The emperor kept his head bowed;
He stroked his beard and smoothed his moustache.   215
He replied neither for nor against his nephew;
The Franks stay quiet, except for Ganelon.
He rises to his feet and came before Charles,
Beginning his speech with great ferocity.

220 He said to the king: 'Trust a fool and you will regret it,
Whether myself or another, except to your advantage.
When King Marsile sends you word
That with his hands clasped in yours he will become your vassal
And hold all Spain from you as a gift,
225 And then receive the faith we hold,
He who advises that we should reject this pact,
Does not care, lord, what sort of death we die.
Arrogant advice should not prosper;
Let us avoid fools and heed the wise.'   AOI.

16

230 It was Naimes who next came forward;
There was no better vassal in the court than he.
He said to the king: 'You have heard these words;
Count Ganelon has made this reply to you.
There is sense in it, if it be properly understood;
235 King Marsile is defeated in war.
You have taken all his castles;
With your catapults you have shattered his walls,
Burned his cities and conquered his men.
When he asks you to have mercy on him,
240 It would be a sin to proceed . . .
Since he wishes to reassure you with hostages,
This great war should not continue.'
The Franks say: 'The duke has spoken well.'   AOI.

17

'My lord barons, whom shall we send
245 To King Marsile in Saragossa?'
Duke Naimes replies: 'I shall go, with your consent.
Hand me the glove and the staff.'
The king answers: 'You are a wise man;
By this beard and this moustache of mine,
250 You will not go so far from me this year.
Sit down, since no one calls you forth.'

18

'My lord barons, whom can we send
To the Saracen who holds Saragossa?'
Roland replies: 'I am prepared to go.'
'You certainly will not,' said Count Oliver,   255
'Your temperament is most hostile and fierce,
I am afraid you might pick a quarrel.
If the king wishes, I am prepared to go.'
The king answers: 'Be silent, both of you;
Neither you nor he will set foot there.   260
By this white beard of mine which you see,
The twelve peers are not to be nominated.'
The Franks stay quiet, well and truly silenced.

19

Turpin of Reims then rose from the ranks
And said to the king: 'Let your Franks be.   265
You have been in this country for seven years;
They have endured many troubles and toils.
Give me, lord, the staff and the glove
And I shall go to the Spanish Saracen
To see what lies behind his outward show.'   270
The emperor responds angrily:
'Go and be seated on that white silk cloth;
Do not say another word, unless I bid you to.'   AOI.

20

'Noble knights,' said the Emperor Charles,
'Choose someone for me from my domain   275
To carry my message to Marsile.'
Roland said: 'It will be Ganelon, my stepfather.'
The Franks say: 'He can do this well;
If he is not chosen, no wiser man will be sent.'
Count Ganelon was deeply distressed;   280
He throws down his great marten fur from his shoulders
And stood there in his tunic of silk.

His eyes flashed, his face was very fierce.
His body was noble, his torso broad;
285 So handsome was he that all his peers gaze at him.
He said to Roland: 'You fool, why are you so angry?
Everyone knows that I am your stepfather
And yet you have named me to go to Marsile.
If God grants that I return from there,
290 I shall stir up against you such a great feud
That it will last for the rest of your life.'
Roland replies: 'I hear arrogant and foolish words;
Everyone knows that I fear no threats.
But it must be a wise man who delivers the message.
295 If the king desires it, I am ready to perform the task for you.'

21

Ganelon replies: 'You will not go in my place;   AOI.
You are not my vassal and I am not your lord.
Charles orders me to carry out his mission.
I shall go to Marsile in Saragossa;
300 I shall perform this somewhat reckless act,
Before giving vent to my great wrath.'*
When Roland heard him, he began to laugh.   AOI.

22

When Ganelon sees that Roland is now laughing at him,
He is so distressed that he almost bursts with rage;
305 He very nearly goes out of his mind.
He says to the count: 'I can no longer love you;
You have nominated me falsely.
Rightful emperor, see me standing here before you;
I wish to fulfil your command.'

23

310 'I well know that I must go to Saragossa;   AOI.
Whoever goes there cannot hope to return.
Moreover, I have your sister as my wife

38

And by her I have a son, there could be no finer boy.
His name is Baldwin,' he says, 'and he will become a valiant man.
To him I bequeath my honours and my lands;   315
Take care of him, I shall never set eyes on him again.'
Charles replies: 'You are very soft-hearted;
You must go, since it is my command.'

24

The king said: 'Ganelon, stand forth;   AOI.
Take the staff and the glove.   320
You have heard, the Franks have nominated you.'
'Lord,' said Ganelon, 'this is all Roland's doing;
As long as I live, I shall have no love for him,
Nor Oliver, since he is his companion,
Nor the twelve peers, because they love him so.   325
I challenge them here, lord, in your presence.'
The king said: 'You are of very evil disposition;
You will certainly go, since it is my command.'
'I can go, but without protection: AOI.
Basile had none, nor his brother Basan.'   330

25

The emperor holds out his right glove to him,
But Count Ganelon would rather not have been there;
When he should have received it, it fell to the ground.
The Franks say: 'God, what can this mean?
From this mission great misfortune will befall us.'   335
'Lords,' said Ganelon, 'you will hear more of this.'

26

'Lord,' said Ganelon, 'give me leave;
Since I must go, there is no reason to delay.'
The king said: 'In Jesus's name and mine.'
With his right hand he absolved him and blessed him;   340
Then he handed him the staff and the letter.

39

27

Count Ganelon goes to his lodging.
He begins to put on his armour,
The finest at his disposal.
345 Spurs of gold are fixed upon his feet,
At his side he girds his sword, Murgleis,
And he mounted his warhorse, Tachebrun;
The stirrup was held for him by his uncle Guinemer.
You would have seen so many knights weep there,
350 All of them saying: 'How sad you came here, lord!
You have spent a long time in the king's court
And been recognized by all as a noble vassal;
He who proposed that you should go
Will not be supported or protected by Charlemagne.
355 Count Roland ought not to have thought of this,
Because you are descended from a most noble family.'
Then they say: 'Lord, take us with you.'
Ganelon replies: 'May God forbid!
It is better that I alone die than so many good knights.
360 You will return, lords, to the fair land of France;
Offer greetings to my wife on my behalf
And to Pinabel, my friend and my peer,
And Baldwin, whom you know to be my son.
Help him and regard him as your lord.'
365 He begins his journey and set off on his way.   AOI.

28

Ganelon rides over to a tall olive tree,
He joined the Saracen messengers.
But Blancandrin is waiting for him impatiently;
With great skill they address each other.
370 Blancandrin said: 'Charles is a marvellous man
Who conquered Apulia and all Calabria;
He crossed the salty sea to England
And won the poll-tax for Rome's own use.*
What does he want from us here in our land?'
375 Ganelon replies: 'Such is his nature;
There will never be any man to equal him.'   AOI.

29

Blancandrin said: 'The Franks are most noble men;
Great harm is being done by those dukes and counts
Who give such advice to their lord.
They destroy and torment him and others too.'   380
Ganelon replies: 'In truth I know of no one
Except Roland who will yet be shamed by this.
Yesterday morning the emperor was sitting in the shade;
His nephew came up to him, clad in his coat of mail;
He had been on a forage near Carcassonne.   385
In his hand he held a red apple:
"Here, my lord," said Roland to his uncle,
"I offer you the crowns of each and every king."
His arrogance ought to be his downfall;
For every day he takes risks with his life.   390
If anyone killed him, we should then all have peace.'   AOI.

30

Blancandrin said: 'Roland is a dangerous man
Who wants to make everyone surrender
And who lays claim to every land.
Through which men does he expect to do so much?'   395
Ganelon replies: 'Through the Franks;
They love him so much they will not fail him.
So much gold and silver does he bestow on them.
Mules and war-horses, silks and arms.
The emperor himself is constantly in his thoughts;*   400
For him he will conquer the lands from here to the Orient.'   AOI.

31

Ganelon and Blancandrin rode on,
Until each finally pledged his word
To try to bring about the death of Roland.
On they rode over track and path   405
Until in Saragossa they dismount beneath a yew tree.
A chair of state stood in a pine tree's shade,

Draped in silk from Alexandria.
There sat the king who held all Spain
410 With twenty thousand Saracens all around him.
There is no one who utters or breathed a word,
So keen were they to hear the news.
Here now are Ganelon and Blancandrin.

32

Blancandrin came before Marsile;
415 He held Count Ganelon by the hand
And said to the king: 'May Muhammad protect you
And Apollo too, whose holy laws we keep.
We bore your message to Charles;
He raised both his hands on high
420 And praised his god, but made no other reply.
He sends you one of his noble barons
Who is from France, a rich and powerful man.
From him you will learn if you have peace or not.'
Marsile replies: 'Let him speak, we shall hear him.'   AOI.

33

425 But Count Ganelon had worked everything out;
With great skill he begins to speak,
As a man who knows just what to do.
He said to the king: 'May God protect you,
The Glorious One we must adore.
430 Charlemagne the brave requires
That you receive the holy Christian faith;
He wishes to give you half of Spain as a fief.
If you do not accept this agreement,
You will be captured and bound by force
435 And taken to his domain at Aix
And there condemned to death.
There you will die in shame and dishonour.'
King Marsile was much perturbed by this;
He seized a gold-feathered javelin
440 And would have struck him, had he not been restrained.   AOI.

34

King Marsile changed colour;
He shook the shaft of his javelin.
When Ganelon saw him, his hand went to his sword
And he drew it two fingers' breadth from its sheath,
Saying to it: 'You are most beautiful and fair;   445
I have carried you so long in a king's court
That the Emperor of France will never say
That I died alone in a foreign country
And did not first make the best men pay dearly for you.'
The pagans say: 'Let us break up the quarrel.'   450

35

The finest Saracens all prevailed upon Marsile
To take his seat on the chair of state.
The caliph said: 'You have served us ill
In attempting to strike the Frank.
You ought to have listened to him and heard him out.'   455
'Lord,' said Ganelon, 'it is right for me to suffer this.
I should not fail, for all the gold God made,
Nor for all the wealth in this country,
To tell him, if I am allowed,
That Charles, the mighty king, sends word to him,   460
Through me sends word to him, his mortal foe.'
He is decked in a cloak of sable
Lined with silk from Alexandria.
He flings it down and Blancandrin picks it up.
But he refuses to part with his sword;   465
He held it in his hand by its golden hilt.
The pagans say: 'This is a truly noble man.'   AOI.

36

Ganelon moved closer to the king
And said to him: 'You are wrong to become angry;
For Charles, who holds France, requires   470
That you receive the Christian faith.

He will give you half of Spain as a fief,
The other half will belong to Roland his nephew;
In him you will have a most arrogant partner.
475 If you refuse to accept this accord,
He will lay siege to you in Saragossa.
You will be forcibly captured and bound;
You will be taken straight to his domain at Aix
And have neither palfrey nor war-horse,
480 Nor mule or jenny, on which to ride;
You will be flung upon some wretched pack-horse.
There you will be condemned to lose your head.
Our emperor sends you this letter.'
He passed it over to the pagan's right hand.

37

485 Marsile was white with rage;
He breaks the seal and threw aside the wax.
He looks at the letter and saw the written message:
'Charles, who has France in his power, bids me
Remember the pain and the sorrow
490 Caused by Basan and his brother Basile,
Whose heads I took in the hills of Haltile.
If I wish to redeem my life,
Then I should send him my uncle, the caliph;
Otherwise he will not live in peace with me.'
495 Then Marsile's son spoke to him
And said to the king: 'Ganelon has uttered foolish words.
He has gone so far that he does not deserve to live on;
Give him to me, I shall dispense justice in this matter.'
When Ganelon heard him, he brandished his sword;
500 He leans his back against the pine-tree trunk.

38

The king has entered the garden,
Taking with him his finest men,
And the hoary-headed Blancandrin came

And Jurfaleu, his son and heir,
And the caliph, his uncle, with his vassals.   505
Blancandrin said: 'Summon the Frank;
He has given me his word that he will help our cause.'
The king said: 'You must bring him.'
He took Ganelon by the fingers of his right hand
And leads him to the king in the garden.   510
There they plan the wicked act of treason.   AOI.

39

'My lord Ganelon,' said Marsile to him,
'I acted rather recklessly towards you
In my angry attempt to strike you.
I give you my pledge through these sable furs,   515
Worth more than five hundred pounds in gold,
That before tomorrow night you will be well rewarded.'
Ganelon replies: 'I am not opposed to this;
May God, if it please Him, recompense you.'   AOI.

40

Marsile said: 'Ganelon, trust me when I tell you   520
That it is my wish to be a good friend to you:
I want to hear you speak of Charlemagne.
He is very old and his time is running out;
To my knowledge he is over two hundred years old.
He has travelled through many lands,   525
His buckler has taken so many blows,
So many powerful kings has he reduced to begging.
When will he ever tire of waging war?'
Ganelon replies: 'Charles is not such a man;
No one who sees him or who gets to know him   530
Can fail to say that the emperor is valiant.
I cannot praise or extol him enough,
As there exists no more honour or excellence than his.
Who could relate his great worth?
God has made so much valour shine forth from him   535
That he would rather die than forsake his men.'

41

The pagan said: 'I marvel greatly
At Charlemagne, who is old and hoary;
To my knowledge he is more than two hundred years old.
540 His body has suffered in so many lands,
So many blows has he taken from lance and spear,
So many powerful kings has he reduced to begging.
When will he ever tire of waging war?'
'Never,' said Ganelon, 'as long as his nephew lives;
545 There is no such man beneath the vault of heaven.
His companion Oliver is very brave;
The twelve peers, whom Charles loves so much,
Form the vanguard with twenty thousand knights;
Charles is secure, because he fears no man.'   AOI.

42

550 The Saracen said: 'Great is my amazement
At Charlemagne, who is hoary and white-haired;
To my knowledge he is more than two hundred years old.
He has been victorious in so many lands,
So many blows has he taken from good sharp spears,
555 So many powerful kings has he vanquished in battle.
When will he ever tire of waging war?'
'Never,' said Ganelon, 'as long as Roland is alive;
There is no such man from here to the Orient.
Oliver, his companion, is very brave.
560 The twelve peers, whom he loves so much,
Form the vanguard with twenty thousand Franks;
Charles is secure, he fears no man alive.'   AOI.

43

'My lord Ganelon,' said Marsile the king,
'My army is such that you will never see finer;
565 I have at my disposal four hundred thousand men.
With them can I do battle with Charles and the Franks?'
Ganelon replies: 'You cannot do so at this time:
You would suffer heavy losses amongst your pagans.

Avoid foolishness, stick to common sense.
Give the emperor such great wealth   570
That all the Franks will be absolutely astonished;
Through the twenty hostages which you would send him,
The king will go back to the fair land of France.
He will leave his rearguard behind him;
In it will be his nephew, Count Roland, I believe,   575
And Oliver, the brave and the courtly.
The counts are doomed to die, if I am believed;
Charles will see his great pride fall.
He will never again have the heart to do battle with you.'   AOI.

44

'My lord Ganelon,' said King Marsile,   580
'How can I bring about Roland's death?'
Ganelon replies: 'I can tell you how.
The king will be at the main pass of Cize;
He will have stationed the rearguard behind him.
In it will be his nephew, Count Roland the powerful,   585
And Oliver in whom he places so much trust.
They have twenty thousand Franks in their company;
Send a hundred thousand of your pagans against them.
Let these men join battle with them at the start;
The Frankish army will be crippled and battered.   590
There will be, I do not deny, losses amongst your men;
Offer battle again in the same way.
Whatever happens, Roland will not escape.
Then you will have performed a noble act of chivalry;
You will have no more war as long as you live.   AOI.   595

45

'If anyone could bring about Roland's death,
Then Charles would lose the right arm from his body,
And those fearsome armies would fight no more.
Charles would never again assemble such great forces;
The great land would remain in peace.'   600

47

When Marsile hears him, he kissed his neck;
Then he begins to open up his treasures.   AOI.

46

Marsile said: 'Why should we discuss this further?
Advice is not worthy in which one . . .
605 You will swear to me that you will betray Roland.'
Ganelon replies: 'Let it be as you please.'
On the relics in his sword Murgleis
He swore the treason and committed his crime.   AOI.

47

A lectern stood there, made of ivory;
610 Marsile has a book brought forward,
Containing the law of Muhammad and Tervagant.
This is what the Spanish Saracen swore:
That if he finds Roland in the rearguard,
He will do battle against him with all his men,
615 And, if possible, Roland will surely die there.
Ganelon replies: 'May your will be done.'   AOI.

48

Then a pagan Valdabrun came forward,
He stands before King Marsile.
Laughing loudly, he said to Ganelon:
620 'Hold my sword, no man has one finer;
There are over a thousand gold mangons in its hilt.
As a mark of friendship, my lord, I give it you,
For your help over the valiant Roland,
So that we can find him in the rearguard.'
625 'This will certainly be done,' replies Count Ganelon;
Then they kissed each other on the face and the chin.

49

Then a pagan, Climborin, came forward.
Laughing loudly, he said to Ganelon:
'Take my helmet, I have never seen finer . . .
And help us with regard to Roland the marquis,   630
Show us how we can bring shame upon him.'
'This will certainly be done,' replied Ganelon.
Then they kissed each other on the mouth and the face.   AOI.

50

Then Queen Bramimonde came forward:
'I love you dearly, lord,' she said to the count,   635
'For my lord and his men hold you in very high esteem.
I shall send your wife two necklaces,
Made of gold and full of amethysts and jacinths;
They are worth more than all the wealth in Rome.
Your emperor has never seen their like.'   640
He took them and pushes them into his boots.   AOI.

51

The king summons Malduit, his treasurer:
'Has Charles's gift of money been made ready?'
And he replies: 'Yes, lord, in abundance;
Seven hundred camels, laden with gold and silver,   645
And twenty of the noblest hostages on earth.'   AOI.

52

Marsile clasped Ganelon by the shoulder
And said to him: 'You are most valiant and wise.
By the most sacred faith which you hold,
Mind you do not turn your heart away from us.   650
I intend to give you a great deal of my wealth,
Ten mules laden with the finest Arabian gold.
No year will pass without my offering you the same;
Take the keys to this vast city,

655 Present this great treasure to King Charles,
Then have Roland appointed for me to the rearguard.
If I can find him in pass or defile,
I shall engage him in mortal combat.'
Ganelon said: 'I think I have delayed too long.'
660 Then he mounted and sets off on his journey.   AOI

53

The emperor is drawing closer to home;
He has reached the city of Galne.
Count Roland captured and destroyed it;
From that day forth for a hundred years it lay deserted.
665 The king awaits news of Ganelon
And the tribute from the great land of Spain.
At dawn, just as day breaks,
Count Ganelon arrived back at camp.   AOI

54

The emperor arose early;
670 The king heard mass and matins.
He stood on the green grass before his tent;
Roland was there and Oliver the valiant,
Duke Naimes and many others.
Ganelon came, the traitor, the perjurer;
675 He begins to speak with great cunning
And he said to the king: 'May God protect you.
I bring you here the keys of Saragossa;
From there I bring you great riches
And twenty hostages, guard them well.
680 And Marsile the valiant sends you this message:
You must not reproach him because of the caliph,
For before my eyes I saw four hundred thousand armed men,
Clad in hauberks, some with helmets laced,
Their swords, with pommels inlaid with gold, girt about them,
685 Who escorted him down to the sea.
They are fleeing from Marsile because of Christianity

Which they do not wish to uphold or maintain.
Before they had sailed four leagues
A storm and violent wind overtook them;
There they drowned, never will you see them again.　690
If he were alive, I should have brought him.
As for the pagan king, lord, rest assured,
You will not see this first month pass
Without his following you to the kingdom of France;
And he will receive the faith which you hold.　695
With his hands clasped in yours he will be your vassal;
From you he will hold the kingdom of Spain.'
The king said: 'Thanks be to God.
You have done well, your reward will be great.'
Throughout the army they have a thousand bugles sounded;　700
The Franks break camp and load up their pack-horses;
Towards the fair land of France they have all set off.　AOI.

55

Charlemagne has laid waste Spain,
Taken the castles and ravaged the cities.
The king says that his war is over;　705
Towards the fair land of France the emperor rides.
Count Roland fixed the standard to his lance
And raised it skyward on a hilltop.
The Franks pitch camp throughout the countryside;
The pagans ride through the great valleys,　710
Clad in hauberks and . . .
With helmets laced and swords girt about them,
Shields slung around their necks and lances decked.
They come to rest in a wood on the mountain top.
Four hundred thousand await the break of day.　715
O God, how sad! The Franks know nothing of it!　AOI.

56

The day passes, the night grows dark;
Charles, the mighty emperor, lies asleep.
He dreamed he was at the main pass of Cize;

51

720 In his hands he was holding his lance of ash.
Count Ganelon seized it from his grasp;
He broke it and brandished it with such violence
That the splinters flew up into the sky.
Charles sleeps on without being roused. AOI.

57

725 After this dream he had another vision:
That he was in France in his chapel at Aix;
In his right arm he is bitten by a vicious boar.
From the direction of the Ardennes he saw a leopard coming;
It attacks his body with great ferocity.
730 From within the hall a hunting-dog came down,
Bounding and leaping towards Charles.
It tore off the right ear of the first boar;
Angrily it wrestles with the leopard.
The Franks say that there is a mighty battle;
735 They do not know which of them will win it.
Charles sleeps on without being roused.

58

The night passes and the clear dawn appears.
Amidst the host the bugles sound.
The emperor rides most fiercely.
740 'Lord barons,' said the emperor Charles,
'See the passes and the narrow defiles;
Nominate someone for me to be in the rearguard.'
Ganelon replies: 'Roland, this stepson of mine;
You have no more valiant man than he.'
745 When the king hears him, he stares fiercely at him,
And said to him: 'You are the living devil;
Mortal rage has entered your body.
And who will be in the vanguard before me?'
Ganelon replies: 'Ogier of Denmark;
750 You have no one who will do it better than he.'

59

Count Roland, when he heard himself nominated,   AOI.
Then spoke like a true knight:
'Lord stepfather, it is my duty to love you.
You have appointed me to the rearguard;
Charles, the king who holds France, will not lose,   755
I warrant, a single palfrey or war-horse,
Nor mule or jenny, which is fit to ride,
And he will not lose a single pack-horse or sumpter
Without its first being purchased by the sword.'
Ganelon replies: 'You speak the truth, as I well know.'   AOI.   760

60

When Roland hears that he was to be in the rearguard,
He spoke angrily to his stepfather:
'Ah, wretch, base and low-born man;
Did you think that I would drop the gauntlet,
As you dropped the staff in front of Charles?'   AOI.   765

61

'Rightful emperor,' said Roland the valiant,
'Give me the bow which you hold in your grasp.
I warrant they will not rebuke me
For dropping it, as Ganelon did,
From his right hand, when he received the staff.'   770
The emperor kept his head down
And stroked his beard and twisted his moustache.
He cannot prevent his eyes from shedding tears.

62

After this Naimes came forward;
A better vassal than he was not to be found at court.   775
He said to the king: 'You have heard this clearly;
Count Roland is very angry;
He has been appointed to the rearguard.

You have no one who could ever change this;
780 Give him your well-stretched bow
And provide him with able companions.'
The king gives him the bow and Roland received it.

63

The emperor calls his nephew Roland:
'Fair nephew, now understand me truly;
785 I shall leave you the gift of half my army.
Retain them, this will be your salvation.'
Roland made this reply: 'I shall do no such thing.
May God confound me, if I dishonour my family.
I shall retain twenty thousand most valiant Franks;
790 Proceed through the passes with confidence.
You need fear no one in my lifetime.'

64

Count Roland mounted his war-horse.   AOI.
His companion Oliver comes up to him;
Gerin came and the worthy Count Gerer
795 And Oton came up and Berenger too
And up came Astor and Anseis the fierce.
Gerard of Roussillon, the old, came,
And the mighty Duke Gaifier has come.
The archbishop said: 'I shall go, by my head!'
800 'And I with you,' said Count Gautier;
'I am Roland's vassal, I must not fail him.'
From amongst themselves they select twenty thousand
    knights.   AOI.

65

Count Roland addresses Gautier del Hum:
'Take a thousand Franks from our land of France
805 And occupy the defiles and the heights,
So that the emperor will not lose a single man.'   AOI.

Gautier replies: 'For you I must do this well.'
With a thousand Franks from their land of France
Gautier patrols the defiles and the heights.
Bad news will not drive him down,   810
Before seven hundred swords have been unsheathed.
King Almari from the kingdom of Belferne
Joined battle with them that wretched day.

66

High are the hills and the valleys dark.
The rocks dull-hued, the defiles filled with horror.   815
The Franks spent the day in great sorrow;
You could hear the noise for fifteen leagues around.
When they reach the mighty land,
They saw Gascony, the land of their lord,
Then they are reminded of their fiefs and their honours,   820
Of maidens and their noble wives.
There is no one who is not moved to tears.
More than all the rest Charles is full of anguish;
In the Spanish pass he has left his nephew.
Emotion assails him; he cannot hold back his tears.   AOI.   825

67

The twelve peers have remained in Spain.
In their company they have twenty thousand Franks;
They are not afraid and have no terror of dying.
The emperor is returning to France;
Beneath his cloak he gives vent to his feelings.   830
Duke Naimes rides beside him
And he says to the king: 'What is weighing on your mind?'
Charles replies: 'It is wrong to ask me;
My distress is so great, I cannot but lament it.
France will be destroyed by Ganelon.   835
Last night an angelic vision came to me
That in my hands my lance was broken by the man
Who had nominated my nephew to the rearguard.

I have left him in a foreign land;
840 God! If I lose him, I shall never replace him.'   AOI.

68

Charlemagne cannot hold back his tears;
A hundred thousand Franks feel great pity for him
And terrible dread for Roland.
The evil Ganelon has committed treason;
845 He has had great gifts from the pagan king,
Gold and silver, silks and brocades,
Mules and horses, camels and lions.
Marsile summons the barons of Spain,
Counts, viscounts, dukes and almaçors,
850 The emirs and the sons of lesser counts.
In three days he assembles four hundred thousand men.
In Saragossa he has the drums beaten;
They hoist Muhammad on high in the tallest tower.
No pagan fails to pray to him and adore him.
855 Then they ride with great zeal
Through Tere Certaine, the valleys and the hills.
They saw the ensigns of the men of France.
The rearguard with the twelve companions
Will not fail to join battle with them.

69

860 The nephew of Marsile came forward,
On a mule which he spurred on with a staff.
He said to his uncle with a smile:
'My lord king, I have served you so long,
And I have known pain and suffering;
865 I have fought victoriously in the field.
Grant me a boon: that is to strike at Roland first.
I shall kill him with my sharp spear;
If Muhammad is willing to be my protector,
I shall redeem every portion of Spain,
870 From the Spanish passes right up to Durestant.

Charles will be weary and his Franks will give up.
Never will you have war as long as you live.'
King Marsile gave him the gauntlet.   AOI.

70

Marsile's nephew holds the gauntlet in his hand.
He addresses his uncle in very fierce terms: 875
'My lord king, you have granted me a boon.
Select twelve of your barons for me
And I shall join battle with the twelve companions.'
First to respond is Falsaron;
He was the brother of King Marsile: 880
'Fair nephew, you and I shall go;
We shall engage in this battle well and truly.
The rearguard of Charles's great army
Is destined to be slaughtered by us.'   AOI.

71

King Corsalis rides up from the other side;   885
He is a Berber and well versed in the black arts.
He spoke in the fashion of a good vassal;
For all God's gold he would not become a coward.
Here comes Malprimis of Brigant, spurring on his horse;
He can run faster than any horse.   890
Before Marsile he cries out loudly:
'I shall go to Rencesvals;
If I find Roland, I shall not fail to lay him low.'

72

An emir is there from Balaguer.
His body is very handsome and his face fierce and fair.   895
When he is mounted on his horse,
He bears his arms with great ferocity.
He is well known for his courage;
Had he been a Christian, he would have been a worthy baron.

900　Before Marsile he made his cry:
　　　'To Rencesvals I shall go;
　　　If I find Roland, he will end up dead,
　　　And so will Oliver and all the twelve peers.
　　　The Franks will die in sorrow and shame;
905　Charlemagne is old and in his dotage.
　　　He will be weary of waging his war
　　　And Spain will remain in our power.'
　　　King Marsile thanked him warmly.　　　　　　　　　　　AOI.

73

　　　An almaçor is there from Moriane;
910　No one in the land of Spain is more treacherous.
　　　Before Marsile he made his boast:
　　　'To Rencesvals I shall lead my company,
　　　Twenty thousand men with shields and lances.
　　　If I find Roland, he is assured of death;
915　No day will pass without Charles lamenting him.'　　　AOI.

74

　　　On the other side is Turgis of Turteluse;
　　　He is a count and the city is his.
　　　His ambition is to slaughter Christians;
　　　He joins the others in front of Marsile.
920　He said to the king: 'Never be dismayed.
　　　Muhammad is worth more than Saint Peter of Rome;
　　　If you serve him, victory will be ours.
　　　I shall go and do battle with Roland at Rencesvals;
　　　No one will protect him from death.
925　See my sword which is fine and long;
　　　I shall put it to use against Durendal.
　　　You will hear very clearly which will win the day;
　　　The Franks will die, if they risk battle with us.
　　　Charles the old will have sorrow and shame;
930　Never will he wear his crown on earth.'

75

On another side is Escremiz of Valterne;
He is a Saracen and that land is his.
In front of Marsile he cries out in the throng:
'To Rencesvals I shall go, to shatter pride.
If I find Roland, he will cease to bear his head   935
And Oliver too, who commands all the rest;
The twelve peers are doomed to perish.
The Franks will die and France will be bereft;
Charles will lack good vassals.'   AOI.

76

A pagan Estorgans is there too,   940
And so is Estramariz, his companion.
They are felons, wretched traitors.
Marsile says: 'Lords, come forward.
You will go to the passes of Rencesvals
And you will help to lead my men.'   945
And they reply: 'At your command.
We shall attack Oliver and Roland;
The twelve peers will not escape death,
Our swords are fine and sharp;
We shall stain them red with warm blood.   950
The Franks will die, Charles will be full of sorrow;
We shall present you with their mighty land.
Come along with us, king, and see for yourself;
We shall make a present of the emperor to you.'

77

Margariz of Seville came galloping up;   955
He holds the land right up to Cazmarines.
He is so handsome that the ladies adore him;
Whenever one sees him, her eyes light up.
When she catches sight of him, she becomes all smiles.
No pagan is such a good knight;   960
He came and joined the throng, crying out above the rest

And saying to the king: 'Do not be dismayed.
I shall go to Rencesvals to kill Roland
And Oliver will not escape with his life.
965 The twelve peers have stayed behind to become martyrs.
Look at my sword with its hilt of gold;
It was a present from the emir of Primes.
I pledge to you that it will be plunged into red blood.
The Franks will die and France will be shamed;
970 Charles the old with the hoary-white beard,
Will never know a day without sorrow and grief.
Within a year we shall have France in our power;
We can lie in the town of Saint-Denis.'
The pagan king bows low before him.   AOI.

78

975 Chernubles of Munigre is there as well.
His hair sweeps down to the ground.
When at play, he can carry a heavier weight for sport,
Than four mules can bear, when they are carrying a burden.
In the land, it is said, whence he came,
980 The sun does not shine and wheat cannot grow,
Rain does not fall nor dew collect.
There is no stone which is not completely black.
Some say that devils live there.
Chernubles says: 'My fine sword is girt about me.
985 In Rencesvals I shall stain it red;
If I find Roland, the brave, in my path,
My word is never to be believed, if I fail to attack him.
With my sword I shall overcome Durendal;
The Franks will die and France will be bereft.'
990 At these words the twelve peers assemble.
They take along with them a hundred thousand Saracens
Who hasten eagerly towards the fight;
They arm themselves in a grove of pines.

79

The pagans arm themselves with Saracen hauberks,
Most of which are triple linked. 995
They lace on their fine helmets from Saragossa
And gird themselves with swords of steel from Viana.
They have shields which are fair and spears from Valence,
And pennons which are white, blue and red.
Leaving their mules and all their palfreys 1000
They mount their war-horses and ride in close array.
The day was fine and the sun bright;
They have no equipment which does not gleam in the light.
They sound a thousand trumpets to enhance the effect.
The noise is great and the Franks heard it. 1005
Oliver said: 'Lord companion, I think
We may have a battle with the Saracens.'
Roland replies: 'And may God grant it to us.
It is our duty to be here for our king:
For his lord a vassal must suffer hardships 1010
And endure great heat and great cold;
And he must lose both hair and hide.
Now let each man take care to strike great blows,
So that no one can sing a shameful song about us.
The pagans are wrong and the Christians are right. 1015
No dishonourable tale will ever be told about me.' AOI.

80

Oliver is on a lofty hilltop.
He looks down to the right over a grassy vale
And he sees the approach of the pagan army.
He called to Roland, his companion: 1020
'Over towards Spain I can see the glint of burnished steel,
So many shining hauberks and gleaming helmets.
These men will cause our Franks great sorrow;
Ganelon was aware of this, the felon, the traitor,
He who appointed us before the emperor.' 1025
'Be silent, Oliver,' replies Count Roland,
'He is my stepfather; I want no word said about him.'

81

Oliver has climbed a hill.
Now he has a clear view of the kingdom of Spain
1030 And of the Saracens assembled in such numbers.
Their hauberks, studded with gold and gems, gleam
Like their shields and saffron helmets
And their spears with pennons fixed.
On his own he cannot count the divisions;
1035 They are too numerous for him to measure their extent.
And he himself is greatly disturbed;
With all speed he came down the hill,
Approached the Franks and told them everything.

82

Oliver said: 'I have seen pagans;
1040 Never has any man on earth seen more.
A hundred thousand men with shields make up the van,
With helmets laced and clad in gleaming hauberks,
Their lances erect and burnished spears aglow.
You will have a battle, never has there been one such.
1045 Frankish lords, may God grant you strength;
Stand firm, lest we should be defeated.'
The Franks say: 'A curse on him who flees.
No one of us will fail you for fear of death.'   AOI.

83

Oliver said: 'There is a huge army of pagans,
1050 But mighty few of our Franks, it seems to me.
Companion Roland, blow your horn;
Charles will hear it and the army will turn back.'
Roland replies: 'That would be an act of folly;
Throughout the fair land of France I should lose my good name.
1055 Straightway I shall strike great blows with Durendal;
Right up to its golden hilt the blade will run with blood.
These treacherous pagans will rue the day they came to this pass.
I swear to you, they are all condemned to death.'   AOI.

84

'Companion Roland, blow your horn;
Charles will hear it and turn the army round.   1060
With his barons the king will come to our aid.'
Roland replies: 'God forbid that
My kinsmen should incur reproach because of me
Or that the fair land of France should fall into disrepute.
No, I shall strike many a blow with Durendal,   1065
My good sword, which is girt about me;
You will see the entire blade all smeared with blood.
These treacherous pagans will rue the day they gathered here.
I swear to you, all are doomed to die.'   AOI.

85

'Companion Roland, blow your horn;   1070
Charles will hear it, as he rides through the pass.
I swear to you, the Franks will soon return.'
'God forbid,' replies Roland to him,
'That any man alive should say that
Pagans made me blow the horn;   1075
My kinsmen will never have to bear that reproach.
When I enter into the thick of the battle,
I shall strike one thousand and seven hundred blows;
You will see the steel blade of Durendal covered in blood.
The Franks are brave men, they will strike courageously;   1080
For those from Spain there will be no escape from death.'

86

Oliver said: 'I see no blame in this.
I have seen the Saracens from Spain;
The valleys and the mountains are covered with them,
The hillsides and all the plains.   1085
Vast is the army of this foreign race;
But we have a tiny company of men.'
Roland replies: 'My desire becomes all the greater;
May it never please the Lord God and his angels

1090   That France should ever lose its fame because of me.
       I prefer to die than to suffer such shame;
       For the fine blows we strike the emperor loves us all the more.'

87

       Roland is brave and Oliver is wise;
       Both are marvellous vassals.
1095   Now that they are armed and mounted on their horses,
       Neither will avoid the fray for fear of death.
       The counts are brave and their words lofty;
       The treacherous pagans ride on in great fury.
       Oliver said: 'Roland, just see all this;
1100   The enemy is near us, Charles is so far away.
       You did not deign to blow your horn;
       If the king were here, we should suffer no harm.
       Look up towards the Spanish pass;
       The rearguard, as you see, is in a sorry plight.
1105   Those who are part of this one will never form another.'
       Roland replies: 'Do not speak of such outrage;
       A curse on the heart which cowers in the breast!
       We shall stand firm and hold our ground;
       It is we who shall deal the blows and hack men down.'   AOI.

88

1110   When Roland sees that battle will begin,
       He becomes fiercer than a lion or a leopard.
       He hails the Franks and calls to Oliver:
       'Lord companion, friend, such words should not be spoken;
       The emperor who left the Franks with us
1115   Allotted us twenty thousand men,
       And to his knowledge there was not a coward amongst them.
       For his lord a vassal must suffer great hardship
       And endure both great heat and great cold;
       He must also part with flesh and blood.
1120   Strike with your lance and I with Durendal,
       My good sword, which was a gift from the king.

If I die here, the man who owns it next can say
That it belonged to a noble vassal.'

89

Archbishop Turpin, some way across the field,
Spurs on his horse and gallops up a hill.   1125
With these solemn words he calls upon the Franks:
'Lord barons, Charles has left us here;
For our king we must be prepared to die.
Help us now to sustain the Christian faith.
You will have to engage in battle, as you well know;   1130
For you see the Saracens with your own eyes.
Confess your sins, pray for the grace of God;
To save your souls I shall absolve you all.
If you die, you will be blessed martyrs
And take your place in paradise on high.'   1135
The Franks dismount and kneel upon the ground;
In God's name the archbishop blessed them.
As penance he orders them to strike.

90

The Franks rise and get to their feet;
They are fully absolved and freed of their sins   1140
And the archbishop in God's name has blessed them.
Then they mounted their swift war-horses,
Armed in knightly fashion
And all well equipped for battle.
Count Roland summons Oliver: 1145
'Lord companion, you realized full well
That Ganelon has betrayed us all.
He has accepted gold, riches and money;
It is the emperor's duty to avenge us.
King Marsile has struck a bargain for our lives;   1150
But he will have to pay for it with the sword.'   AOI.

91

Roland has made his way to the Spanish pass,
Riding Veillantif, his good, swift horse.
The arms he bears become him well.
1155 But he brandishes his spear,
And turns its point towards the sky,
A pure white pennon fixed upon its tip,
And its golden streamers fluttering down upon his hands.
His body is noble, his face fair and smiling;
1160 His companion follows close behind
And the Franks hail him as their protector.
Towards the Saracens he looks fiercely
And humbly and tenderly towards the Franks.
And he addressed them in courtly fashion:
1165 'My lord barons, gently, not too fast!
These pagans are heading for great slaughter;
Today our spoils will be fine and noble.
No king of France has ever had such wealth.'
At these words the armies come together.   AOI.

92

1170 Oliver said: 'I have no desire to speak.
You did not deign to sound your oliphant
So you receive no help at all from Charles.
He knows nothing of this and shares no guilt;
Those who remain with him are not to blame.
1175 Now ride for all you are worth;
My lord barons, hold your ground in the field.
In God's name, I beg you, let it be your resolve
To strike blows, to give and to receive;
We must not forget Charles's battle-cry.'
1180 At these words the Franks cried out.
Anyone who heard the call of 'Monjoie'
Would have been reminded of true courage.
Then they ride, O God, with such great zest;
They spur on their horses with vigour to speed upon their way.
1185 And they go to strike; what else were they to do?

But the Saracens had no dread of them;
See now, Franks and pagans joined in battle.

93

Marsile's nephew, whose name is Aelroth,
Is first to ride out before the host.
He hurls insulting words at our Franks: 1190
'Treacherous Franks, you will join battle with us today;
He who should have protected you has betrayed you;
The king is a fool to have left you in the pass.
Today the fair land of France will lose its fame
And Charlemagne the right hand from his body.'   1195
When Roland hears these words, O God, what anger!
He spurs on his horse, lets it race ahead;
The count rides on to strike him with all his might.
He breaks his shield and tears his hauberk open;
He splits his breast and shatters all his bones,   1200
Severing from his back his entire spine.
With his spear he casts forth his soul,
And, giving him a firm push, makes his body topple.
With a free blow of his lance he flings him dead from his horse;*
He has broken his neck in two.   1205
He will not forgo, he says, the chance to rail at him:
'You utter wretch, Charles is no fool
And never a man to care for treachery.
He acted properly in leaving us in the pass;
Today the fair land of France will not lose its fame.   1210
Strike, Franks, the first blow is ours!
We are right, but these wretches are wrong.'   AOI.

94

A duke is there, his name is Falsaron;
He was brother to King Marsile.
He held the land of Dathan and Abiram;   1215
No more foul traitor exists upon this earth.
Between his eyes his brow was spread so broad

Its measure was a good half-foot.
His grief is great to see his nephew slain;
1220 He breaks out from the throng, intent upon a fight,
And shouts the pagan battle-cry.
Towards the Franks he hurls these mocking words:
'This day the fair land of France will lose its honour.'
Oliver hears him and is greatly enraged.
1225 He urges on his horse with his golden spurs
And goes to strike him in courageous fashion.
He breaks his shield and rends his hauberk,
Ramming the tails of his pennon right into his body.
With a free blow of his lance he flings him dead from his saddle.
1230 Looking down, he sees the wretch lying there
And addressed him in ferocious terms:
'I am not hindered, villain, by your threats;
Strike, Franks, for we shall vanquish them with ease.'
He shouts 'Monjoie', the battle-cry of Charles.   AOI.

95

1235 A king is there whose name is Corsablix;
He is a Berber from a foreign land.
He called to the other Saracens:
'This is a battle we can handle well,
For the Franks are very few in number.
1240 Those who are here deserve our contempt;
Charles will not protect a single one.
This is the day on which they must die.'
Archbishop Turpin heard these words clearly;
No man on earth does he hate more;
1245 He urges on his horse with his spurs of pure gold
And went to strike him with great strength;
He shattered his shield, destroyed his hauberk
And plunged his great spear right through his body.
He gives him a firm push and sends him reeling to his death;
1250 With a free blow of his lance he flings him dead on the ground.
He looks back and sees the wretch sprawling there;
He will not forgo, he says, the chance to rail at him:

'Vile pagan, you have told a lie;
Charles, my lord, will always guard us well.
Our Franks have no desire to flee;   1255
All your companions will be laid to rest by us.
My news is this: you must suffer death.
Strike, Franks, let no one forget his duty.
This first blow is ours, thank God.'
He shouts 'Monjoie' to hold the field.   1260

96

And Gerin strikes Malprimis of Brigal;
His fine shield is not worth a penny.
He shatters its crystal boss
And sends one half flying to the ground.
He rends his hauberk right down to his flesh   1265
And plunges his fine spear deep into his body.
The pagan falls to the ground in a heap;
His soul is carried off by Satan.   AOI.

97

And his companion Gerer strikes the emir;
He breaks his shield and shatters the mail of his hauberk.   1270
He plunges his fine spear into his entrails,
Gives him a firm push and forces it right through him.
He flings him dead on the field with a free blow of his lance.
Oliver said: 'Our battle is a noble one.'

98

Duke Samson goes to strike the almaçor.   1275
He broke his shield wrought with gold and flowers;
His fine hauberk offers him no protection.
He pierces his heart, his liver and his lungs,
Flinging him dead, no matter whom it grieves.
The archbishop said: 'This is a baron's blow!'   1280

THE SONG OF ROLAND

99

Then Anseis gives his horse full rein
And goes to strike Turgis of Turteluse.
He breaks his shield beneath its golden boss
And smashed the lining of his hauberk.
1285 He plunges the point of his fine spear into his body.
He gave him a firm push and rammed the iron right through him;
With a free blow of his lance he lays him out dead on the ground.
Roland said: 'This is a brave man's blow!'

100

And Engeler, the Gascon from Bordeaux,
1290 Spurs on his horse and gives it full rein.
He goes to strike Escremiz of Valterne,
Breaking and shattering the shield around his neck.
He smashed the ventail on his hauberk
And strikes him right in the centre of his breast.
1295 With a free blow of his lance he flings him dead from his saddle;
Then he said to him: 'You have met your end.'   AOI.

101

And Oton* strikes a pagan Estorgans
On the upper rim of his shield,
Hacking away all the red and white paint.
1300 He has torn off the skirts of his hauberk
And plunges his fine, sharp spear into his body,
Flinging him dead off his swift horse.
Then he said: 'You will never be saved.'

102

And Berenger strikes Astramariz;
1305 He broke his shield and destroyed his hauberk.
He plunged his strong spear right through his body,
Flinging him dead amongst a thousand Saracens.
Ten of the twelve peers are slain

And now only two remain alive.
They are Chernubles and Count Margariz.   1310

103
Margariz is a very valiant knight,
Handsome, strong, swift and nimble.
He spurs on his horse and goes to strike Oliver;
He breaks his shield beneath the pure gold boss
And his thrusting spear shaved his side.   1315
God prevented a wound to his body.
He smashes Oliver's lance, but does not unhorse him;
Without hindrance he goes on his way.
He sounds his bugle to rally his men.

104
The battle is terrible and now joined by all.   1320
Count Roland is no laggard;
He strikes with his spear, while the shaft still lasts.
With fifteen blows he has broken and destroyed it;
He draws forth Durendal, his fine, naked sword,
And spurs on his horse to strike at Chernubles.   1325
He breaks his helmet with its gleaming carbuncles,
Slices off his coif and his scalp,
As well as slicing through his eyes and his face,
His shining hauberk with its close-meshed mail
His whole body right down to his crotch,   1330
And right into his saddle which is of beaten gold;
His sword came to rest in the horse itself.
He slices through its spine, seeking no joint,
And flinging them both dead in the meadow on the lush grass.
Then he said to him: 'Villain, you set out to meet your doom;   1335
You will receive no help from Muhammad.
A wretch like you will not win today's battle.'

105

Count Roland rides through the battlefield;
He holds Durendal, which cuts and cleaves so well,
1340 And wreaks great havoc amongst the Saracens.
What a sight to see body piled upon body
And all the clear blood spilled all around!
His hauberk and his arms are red with blood,
And so are the neck and shoulders of his fine horse.
1345 Oliver is not sparing with his blows;
The twelve peers deserve no blame
And the Franks hack and hew.
Some pagans die, some are made to faint.
The archbishop said: 'May our barons win!'
1350 He shouts 'Monjoie', the battle-cry of Charles.   AOI.

106

Oliver rides through the thick of the fray;
His lance shaft is broken, only a stump remains.
He goes to strike a pagan, Malun;
He breaks his shield, wrought with gold and flowers,
1355 And smites both his eyes out of his head.
His brains come spilling out over his feet;
He sends him toppling to his death with seven hundred of their
      men.
Then he slew Turgis and Esturguz;
The shaft breaks and shatters right down to his hands.
1360 Roland said to him: 'Companion, what are you doing?
I do not care for a stick in a battle such as this;
Iron and steel should be put to use.
Where is your sword named Halteclere?
Its hilt is of gold and the pommel of crystal.'
1365 'I could not draw it out,' replies Oliver,
'For my need to keep striking was so great.'   AOI.

107

Lord Oliver has drawn forth his fine sword,
Just as his companion Roland insisted,
And he brandished it in knightly fashion.
He strikes a pagan Justin of Val Ferree,   1370
Severing his head right down the middle.
He slices through his body and his saffron byrnie,
His fine saddle, ornamented with gold and gems,
And sliced through his horse's spine.
He flings him dead before him in the meadow.   1375
Roland said: 'I recognize you, brother.
For such blows the emperor loves us.'
On all sides there is a cry of 'Monjoie'.   AOI.

108

Count Gerin sits astride his horse, Sorel,
And his companion, Gerer, on Passecerf.   1380
They loose their reins and both spur on with zest
And go to strike a pagan, Timozel,
One on the shield, the other on the hauberk.
They broke their two spears in his body;
They send him toppling to his death on some fallow land.   1385
I have not heard and do not know
Which of these two was the swifter.
Esperveres, the son of Burdel,
Was slain by Engeler of Bordeaux.*
And the archbishop slew Siglorel,   1390
The enchanter who once visited hell;
Jupiter led him there by sorcery.
Turpin said: 'This man was a criminal.'
Roland replies: 'The villain has met his end.
Oliver, brother, such blows bring me great pleasure.'   1395

109

The battle meanwhile continues to rage;
Franks and pagans strike awesome blows.
Some strike, others defend themselves.

73

How many lances were broken and turned red with blood,
1400 How many pennons, how many ensigns torn,
How many lives of fine young Franks are lost!
Never again will they see their mothers or their wives,
Or the Franks who await them in the pass.   AOI.

110

Charlemagne weeps for them and laments.
1405 To what avail? They will receive no help.
He was ill served that day by Ganelon
Who went to Saragossa to sell his household;
He was later to lose his life and his limbs.
In the trial at Aix he was condemned to hang
1410 And thirty of his relatives with him
Who did not expect to die.   AOI.

111

The battle is awesome and intense.
Oliver and Roland strike mighty blows;
The archbishop deals more than a thousand.
1415 The twelve peers do not hold back
And the Franks strike in unison.
The pagans die in their hundreds and thousands;
Those who do not flee have no escape from death.
Whether they like it or not, they meet their end.
1420 The Franks lose their best defenders;
They will not see their fathers and kinsmen again,
Nor Charlemagne who awaits them in the pass.
In France there is a most terrible storm,
A tempest with thunder and strong winds,
1425 Rain and hail in great quantity.
Lightning strikes again and again
And the whole earth, in truth, begins to quake.
From Saint Michel del Peril to Seinz,
From Besançon to the port of Wissant,
1430 There is no house whose walls do not collapse.

74

At high noon a great darkness gathers;
There is light only when the sky is rent.
No one could see it without a feeling of dread.
Many say: 'It is all over with us;
The end of the world is upon us.'   1435
They do not know it, but their words are wrong;
It is the great sorrow for the death of Roland.

112

The Franks have struck with courage and vigour;
The pagans have died in swarms, by the thousand.
They cannot save two from a hundred thousand.   1440
The archbishop said: 'Our men are very brave;
No one on earth could have better men.
It is written in the Frankish annals
That our emperor has real vassals.'*
Throughout the field they go in search of comrades,   1445
Weeping with grief and pity
For their kinsmen, to whom their heart goes out.
King Marsile rises up against them with his army.   AOI.*

113

Marsile rides through a valley
With his great host which he had assembled.   1450
The king has mustered twenty divisions;
Their helmets, studded with gold and gems, shine bright,
And so do their shields and their saffron byrnies.
Seven thousand bugles sound the charge;
Great is the noise for miles around.   1455
Roland said: 'Oliver, companion, brother,
Ganelon, the traitor, has sworn our death;
The treason can no longer be concealed.
The emperor will exact great revenge.
We shall have a tough and violent battle;   1460
No one has ever seen such an engagement.
I shall strike with my sword, Durendal,

And you, companion, will strike with Halteclere.
We have wielded them in so many places;
1465 We have put an end to so many battles.
No shameful song must be sung about them.'   AOI.

114*

Marsile sees the slaughter of his men
And has his horns and trumpets sounded.
Then he rides with his great assembled host;
1470 Out in front rides a Saracen, Abisme;
He had no greater villain in his company,
A man of evil traits and mighty treachery.
He does not believe in God, the son of the Virgin Mary;
And is as black as molten pitch.
1475 He loves treachery and murder
More than he would love all the gold in Galicia.
No one has ever seen him play or laugh;
He is a man of courage and great zeal
And thereby a friend to Marsile, the treacherous king.
1480 He carries his dragon ensign to which all his men rally.
The archbishop will never care for him;
On seeing him, he wishes to strike him.
Under his breath he says to himself:
'This Saracen appears to me a great heretic;
1485 It is far better for me to strike him dead.
I have never been fond of cowards or cowardice.'   AOI.

115

The archbishop is first to start the battle.
He sits astride the horse he took from Grossaille,
A king whom he killed in Denmark.
1490 The horse is mettlesome and fleet of foot;
Its hooves are hollowed out and its legs flat.
It is short in the haunches and broad in the crupper,
Long in the flank and high along its back;
Its tail is white and its mane yellow,

76

Its ears small and its head tawny.   1495
There is no beast which can match it for pace.
The archbishop spurs on with great valour;
He will not miss this chance to attack Abisme.
He goes to deal him a prodigious blow to the shield
With its precious stones, amethyst and topaz,   1500
Esterminals and blazing carbuncles.
A devil gave this shield to him in Val Metas
And it was presented to him by the emir Galafres.
Turpin strikes it and in no way spares it;
After his blow it is not, I think, worth a penny piece.   1505
He slices him through from one side to the other,
Flinging him dead in an empty spot.
The Franks say: 'This is an act of great valour;
In the archbishop's hands the crozier is truly safe.'

116

The Franks see that there are so many pagans;   1510
On all sides the fields are covered with them.
Time and again they call upon Oliver and Roland
And the twelve peers to act as their protectors.
And the archbishop told them what was on his mind:
'Lord barons, do not indulge in base thoughts;   1515
In God's name I beg you not to flee,
So that no man of worth can sing a shameful song.
It is far better for us to die fighting.
We are promised this: soon we shall meet our end;
Beyond this day we shall cease to be alive.   1520
But in one thing I can act as guarantor:
Holy paradise is open to you;
You will take your seat amongst the Innocents.'
At these words the Franks rejoice;
No one fails to call out 'Monjoie'.   AOI.   1525

117

A Saracen was there from Saragossa;
One half of the city is his.
He is Climborin and he was not a man of worth;
He took the oath from Ganelon the count.
1530 In friendship he kissed him on the mouth
And gave him his helmet and his carbuncle.
He vows to bring the mighty land to shame
And to take away the emperor's crown.
He sits astride his horse called Barbamusche;
1535 It is swifter than a sparrowhawk or swallow.
He spurs on well, giving it free rein,
And goes to strike Engeler of Gascony.
His shield and his byrnie cannot save him;
The pagan plunges the point of his spear into his body,
1540 Gives him a good push, and sends the spear right through him.
With a free blow of his lance, he flings him dead in the field.
Then he shouts: 'These men are easy to destroy;
Strike, pagans, to break up their ranks.'
The Franks say: 'God, what sorrow for such a man!'   AOI.

118

1545 Count Roland calls out to Oliver:
'Lord companion, now Engeler is dead;
We had no more valiant knight than he.'
The count replies: 'May God grant me revenge.'
He urges on his horse with his spurs of pure gold,
1550 Wields Halteclere, whose steel is red with blood,
And with great force goes to strike the pagan.
He dealt his blow and the Saracen falls;
Devils carry off his soul.
Then he slew Duke Alphaien
1555 And next sliced off the head of Escababi.
Seven Arabs were then unhorsed;
They will never again be ripe for battle.
Roland said: 'My companion is enraged;
Compared with mine his deeds deserve great praise.

For such blows Charles holds us more dearly.'   1560
He cries out loud: 'Strike at them, knights.'   AOI.

119

A pagan Valdabrun is also there;
He was raised from the font by King Marsile
And is master of a thousand galleys at sea.
Every sailor claims him as their protector;   1565
He once captured Jerusalem by treachery
And violated the Temple of Solomon,
Slaying the patriarch before the fonts.
He took the oath from Count Ganelon
And gave him his sword and a thousand mangons.   1570
He sits astride his horse called Gramimund,
Which is swifter than a falcon;
He urges him on well with his sharp spurs
And goes to strike the powerful Duke Samson.
He breaks his shield and rends his hauberk,   1575
Ramming the tails of his pennon right into his body.
With a free blow of his lance, he flings him dead from his saddle:
'Strike, pagans, for we shall surely win the day.'
The Franks say: 'God, what sorrow for such a man!'   AOI.

120

Count Roland, when he sees Samson dead,   1580
Was full of grief, as you may well believe.
He spurs on his horse and rides forth at top speed;
He wields Durendal, which is worth more than pure gold,
And with all his might goes to strike him
On the helmet, which was studded with gems and gold.   1585
He slices through his head, his byrnie and his body,
His fine saddle, studded with gold and gems,
And cuts deeply into the back of his horse.
He slays them both, blame or no blame.
The pagans say: 'This is a dreadful blow for us.'   1590
Roland replies: 'I cannot ever love you;
On your side is both pride and wrong.'   AOI.

121

An African was there from Africa;
He is Malquiant, son of King Malcuid.
1595 His equipment is all of beaten gold;
It shines forth to heaven above all others.
He sits astride a horse called Saltperdut;
No beast could beat it for speed.
He goes to strike Anseis on the shield
1600 And hacked right through the red and blue.
He tore off the tails of his hauberk
And plunges the iron and wood deep into his body.
The count is dead, his time is at an end.
The Franks say: 'Baron, how sad that you were here!'

122

1605 Archbishop Turpin rides through the field;
No mass was ever sung by such a priest
Who performed such acts of prowess.
He said to the pagan: 'May God send down evil upon you.
You have slain this man and brought sorrow to my heart.'
1610 He drove his fine horse forward
And struck him square on his shield from Toledo,
Flinging him dead on the green grass.

123

Also there is a pagan, Grandonie,
Son of Capuel, the king of Cappadocia.
1615 He sits astride his horse called Marmorie;
It is swifter than a bird in flight.
He gives it free rein, urges it on with his spurs,
And goes to strike Gerin with all his might.
He breaks his red shield, ripping it from his neck,
1620 Then he split open his byrnie.
He plunges the whole of his blue ensign into him,
Flinging him dead on a high rock.
Next he slays his companion Gerer as well

And Berenger and Guiun from Saint-Antoine.
Then he goes to strike Austorie, a mighty duke,   1625
Who held Valence and fiefs upon the Rhône.
He knocks him down dead: the pagans rejoice.
The Franks say: 'Our men are failing fast.'

124

Count Roland gripped his blood-stained sword;
He had heard clearly that the Franks are lamenting.   1630
So great is his grief that he almost bursts.
He said to the pagan: 'May God inflict woes upon you;
You have slain a man for whom I think you will pay dearly.'
He spurs on his horse, which runs at top speed;
Not caring who pays the price, the two men clash.   1635

125

Grandonie was a valiant and worthy man,
A strong and courageous fighter.
He encountered Roland in his path;
Without having seen him, he recognized him well
From his fierce countenance and his noble body,   1640
His gaze and his whole bearing.
He cannot help but take fright;
He tries to flee, but it is to no avail.
The count strikes him with such power
That he splits his entire helmet down to the nasal   1645
And slices through his nose, his mouth and his teeth,
Through his entire body and his hauberk of Algerian mail,
The two silver bows of his golden saddle
And deep into the horse's back.
Giving them no chance of recovery, he slew them   1650
And all the men of Spain proclaim their great grief.
The Franks say: 'Our protector is striking well.'

125a*

The battle is awesome and violent.
The Franks strike with their burnished swords;
1655 You would have seen so much human grief there,
So many men dead, wounded, soaked in blood,
Men piled upon men, face down or on their backs.
The Saracens can endure it no longer;
Whether they like it or not, they quit the field
1660 And the Franks pursue them hotly.   AOI.

126

The battle is awesome and frenzied;
The Franks strike with vigour and with fury.
They slice through fists, ribs and spines,
And through clothing right down to living flesh.
1665 On to the green grass the clear blood flows down.
. . . .
'Mighty land of France, Muhammad curse you!
Your men are bolder than all others.'
There is no one who fails to cry: 'Marsile!
1670 Ride, king, we are in need of aid.'

127

Count Roland calls out to Oliver:
'Lord companion, I am sure you will agree,
The archbishop is a very fine knight.
There is none better on the face of the earth;
1675 He has great skill in striking with lance and spear.'
The count replies: 'So let us go to his aid.'
With these words the Franks began afresh.
The blows are hard and the battle grievous;
There are heavy losses amongst the Christians.
1680 If you could have seen Roland and Oliver
Hacking and hewing with their swords!
The archbishop strikes with his spear;
Those whom they killed can easily be counted.

It is written in the charters and records,
That, as the annals state, there were four thousand.   1685
In four assaults things went well for them;
But the fifth turns to sorrow and grief.
All the Frankish knights are slain;
No more than sixty were spared by God.
Before they die, they will sell their lives dearly.   AOI.   1690

128

Count Roland sees the heavy losses of his men;
He calls to his companion Oliver:
'Fair lord, dear companion, in God's name, what is your view of
    this?
You see so many fine knights lying on the ground.
We cannot but lament for the fair, sweet land of France;   1695
Of how many men it now stands bereft!
O king, friend, if only you were here.
Oliver, brother, how should we now act?
In what way shall we send him news?'
Oliver said: 'I do not know how to reach him;   1700
I should rather die than have us suffer shame.'   AOI.

129

Roland said: 'I shall sound the oliphant
And Charles, who is going through the pass, will hear it.
I pledge to you, the Franks will soon return.'
Oliver said: 'That would be most shameful   1705
And all your kinsmen would then be blamed;
Such shame would endure as long as they live.
When I spoke to you of this, you did nothing.
But you will not now act so on my advice.
If you sound the horn, there will be no valour in it.   1710
Both your arms are now smeared with blood.'
The count replies: 'I have struck most noble blows.'   AOI.

130

Roland says: 'Our battle is fierce;
I shall sound the horn and King Charles will hear it.'
1715 Oliver said: 'That would not be a courageous act;
When I spoke of this, companion, you did not deign to do it;
If the king had been here, we should have come to no harm.
Those who are there with him deserve no blame.'
Oliver said: 'By this beard of mine;
1720 If ever I see my noble sister Aude,
You will not lie in her arms.'   AOI.

131

Roland said: 'Why do you bear a grudge?'
And he replies: 'Companion, you have been the cause of it.
For a true vassal's act, in its wisdom, avoids folly;
1725 Caution is better than great zeal.
Franks are dead because of your recklessness;
Charles will never again receive our service.
If you had heeded me, my lord would now be here;
We should have fought this battle and won it.
1730 King Marsile would have been captured or killed.
Roland, we can only rue your prowess;
Charlemagne will have no aid from us.
There will be none like him until the Day of Judgement;
You will die here and France will be shamed by it.
1735 Today our loyal comradeship is at its end;
Before evening there will be a sorrowful farewell.'   AOI.

132

The archbishop hears their quarrel.
Urging on his horse, with his spurs of pure gold,
He rode up to them and began to rebuke them:
1740 'Lord Roland and Lord Oliver,
In God's name, I beg you, do not argue.
To blow the horn would be to no avail;
But nevertheless it is now for the best.

Let the king come, then he can avenge our deaths;
The men of Spain must never leave here joyful.   1745
Our Franks will dismount here;
They will find us dead and hacked to pieces
And will raise us on to pack-horses in coffins.
They will shed tears of sorrow and pity for us
And bury us in a church's hallowed ground.   1750
No wolf or pig or dog will devour us.'
Roland replies: 'Lord, you speak well.'   AOI.

133

Roland set the oliphant to his lips.
He takes a firm grip of it and blows with all his might;
The hills are high and the sound travels far.   1755
A full thirty leagues they heard it echo;
Charles heard it and all his companions.
The king said: 'Our men are doing battle.'
But Ganelon made this retort:
'From anyone else, this would have seemed a great untruth.' AOI.   1760

134

Count Roland with pain and distress
Sounds his oliphant in great agony.
The clear blood gushes forth from his mouth
And in his skull the temple bursts.
The sound of the horn which he holds carries far;   1765
Charles hears it, as he makes his way through the pass.
Duke Naimes heard it and the Franks listen to it.
The king said: 'I can hear Roland's horn;
He would never have blown it, if he were not in a fight.'
Ganelon replies: 'There is no battle;   1770
You are old, hoary and white-haired.
Such words make you seem like a child;
You are well aware of Roland's great pride.
It is a wonder that God has stood for it so long.
Once he captured Noples without your orders;   1775

The Saracens poured out from within it
And attacked the good vassal Roland.
Later he cleansed the blood from the meadows with water,
So that no one would see what he had done.
1780 For a mere hare he would blow his horn all day.
Now he is just boasting before his peers;
There is no army on earth who would have dared attack him.
Keep riding; why do you delay?
The great land of France is very far ahead.'   AOI.

135

1785 Count Roland is bleeding from the mouth;
In his skull the temple is burst.
He blows the oliphant with pain and anguish;
Charles heard it and so did the Franks.
The king said: 'The sound of the horn is long drawn out.'
1790 Duke Naimes replies: 'A true vassal makes the effort;
In my estimation there is a battle.
He who wants you to be faint-hearted has betrayed him.
Arm yourself and shout out your battle-cry
And ride to the aid of your noble household.
1795 You can hear clearly the distress cry which Roland sends.'

136

The emperor had his trumpets sounded.
The Franks dismount and arm themselves
With hauberks, helmets and gilded swords.
They have fine shields and spears which are large and sturdy
1800 And white, red and blue pennons.
All the barons in the army mount their horses;
All the way through the pass they spur them on with vigour.
Each says to his neighbour:
'If we could see Roland before he dies,
1805 We should deal great blows together with him.'
What matter? For they have delayed too long.

86

137

The evening sky becomes brighter
And their weapons gleam in the sun;
Hauberks and helmets give off flashes of light,
And so do their shields, which are richly painted with flowers,   1810
And their spears and their gilded pennons.
Full of wrath the emperor rides
And the Franks as well, grieving and sorrowful.
There is no one who does not weep profusely
And they are greatly afraid for Roland.   1815
The king has Count Ganelon seized
And he handed him over to his household cooks.
He summons the master cook, Besgun:
'Guard him for me well, as befits a criminal;
He has betrayed my household.'   1820
The cook takes him and assigns to the task
A hundred scullions, both best and worst.
They pluck out his beard and his moustache
And each gives him four blows with his fist.
They beat him soundly with sticks and staves;   1825
They put an iron collar round his neck
And place him in fetters like a bear.
To his shame they set him upon a pack-horse,
Guarding him until they deliver him to Charles.

138

High are the hills, dark and huge.   AOI.   1830
The valleys are deep and the waters flow swiftly.
They sound their bugles front and rear
And all echo to the oliphant.
The emperor rides with great wrath
And so do the Franks, distressed and sorrowful.   1835
No one fails to weep and show his grief;
They pray to God that he protect Roland,
Until they all arrive upon the battlefield.
Together with him they will strike mighty blows.
What matter? It is to no avail;   1840
They delay too long; they cannot get there in time.   AOI.

139

King Charles rides with great wrath;
Over his byrnie his white beard lies spread.
All the barons of France spur on with zeal;
1845 There is no one who fails to show his sorrow
That they are not with Roland, the captain,
Who is engaged in a fight with the Saracens of Spain.
He is badly hurt; I think his soul can scarce remain.
God! What men are the sixty in his company!
1850 Never did king or captain have finer.   AOI.

140

Roland looks up at the hills and the mountains.
He sees so many of the Franks lying dead
And mourns them like a noble knight:
'Lord barons, may God have mercy on you;
1855 May he grant all your souls a place in paradise
And let them rest amongst celestial flowers.
I have never seen better vassals than you;
You have given me long and faithful service
And conquered such great lands for Charles's use.
1860 How sad that the emperor raised you!
O land of France, you are a most fair country;
Today in such awful ruin you stand bereft.
Frankish barons, I see you dying for me,*
No longer can I protect you or give you succour.
1865 May God, who never lied, aid you;
Oliver, brother, I must not fail you.
I shall die of grief, if nothing else kills me.
Lord companion, let us get back to the fray.'

141

Count Roland returned to the battlefield.
1870 He holds Durendal and strikes like a vassal,
Slicing Faldrun of Pui in two
And twenty-four of their most esteemed fighters.

Never will any man be so bent on vengeance;
Just as a stag flees before the hounds,
So the pagans take flight before Roland.   1875
The archbishop said: 'You act very well.
A knight should have such valour,
Who bears arms and sits astride a good horse.
In battle he should be strong and fierce,
Or else he is not worth four pence.   1880
He ought rather to be a monk in one of those monasteries
And pray all day long for our sins!'
Roland replies: 'Strike, do not spare them.'
At these words the Franks began once more;
There was a heavy loss of Christians.   1885

142

The man who knows no captives will be taken
Puts up a stout defence in such a battle;
So the Franks are as fierce as lions.
Now see, Marsile arrives, like a true baron,
He sits astride his horse called Gaignun.   1890
He spurs it on well and goes to strike Bevon;
He was lord of Beaune and Dijon.
He breaks his shield and rends his hauberk,
Flinging him dead with this one blow.
Then he killed Yvoire and Yvon,   1895
And Gerard of Roussillon along with them.
Count Roland is not far away from him.
He said to the pagan: 'May God bring you misfortune;
With great wrong you kill my companions;
Before we separate you will receive a blow   1900
And learn this day my sword's name.'
He goes to strike him like a baron,
The count slices off his right hand,
Then takes the head from Jurfaleu the Blond;
He was the son of King Marsile.   1905
The pagans cry: 'Help us, Muhammad!
Our gods, avenge us against Charles.

He has sent such villains to this land;
Fear of death will not drive them from the field.'
1910 They said to each other: 'So let us take flight.'
At these words some hundred thousand make off.
Whoever calls them back, they will never return.   AOI.

143

What matter? If Marsile has fled,
There remains behind his uncle Marganice,
1915 Who held Carthage, Alfrere and Garmalie,
And Ethiopia, an accursed land.
He has the black race in his power;
They have large noses and broad ears
And together they number more than fifty thousand men.
1920 They ride fiercely and full of wrath,
Then they shout out the pagan battle-cry.
Roland said: 'Here we shall receive martyrdom
And now I well know we have scarcely any time left.
But a curse on the man who does not first sell himself dear;
1925 Strike, lords, with your polished swords,
And defend your bodies* and your lives,
So that we do not dishonour the fair land of France.
When Charles, my lord, comes to this field,
He will see such slaughter of Saracens
1930 That for every one of us he will find fifteen dead.
He will not fail to bless us.'   AOI.

144

When Roland sees the accursed men,
Who are blacker than ink
And have nothing white save their teeth,
1935 The count said: 'Now I truly know
That we shall die today for certain.
Strike, Franks, for I am beginning afresh!'
Oliver said: 'A curse on the slowest man!'
With these words the Franks return to the fray.

145

When the pagans saw that the Franks were few in number,   1940
They become arrogant and confident.
They said to each other: 'The emperor is wrong.'
Marganice sat astride a sorrel-coloured horse;
He urges it on with his golden spurs
And from behind strikes Oliver right in the back.   1945
He shattered the white hauberk he was wearing
And rammed his lance right through his breast.
Then he says: 'You have received a mighty blow;
Charles left you in the pass for your destruction.
He did us wrong and should not be allowed to boast;   1950
On you alone I have taken ample revenge for our men.'

146

Oliver feels that his wound is mortal.
He grips Halteclere with its burnished steel
And strikes Marganice on his pointed helmet of gold,
Sending its flowers and stones tumbling to the ground.   1955
He slices through his head right down to his front teeth;
Raising his sword on high he flung him down dead.
Then he said: 'Pagan, a curse on you!
I do not deny that Charles has suffered losses;
But to no woman or lady you may have seen   1960
Will you boast, in the kingdom from which you hail,
That you have robbed me of a single penny
Or inflicted any damage on me or anyone else.'
Then he shouts for Roland's help.   AOI.

147

Oliver feels that he has a mortal wound;   1965
Never will he have his fill of vengeance now.
In the thick of the fray he strikes like a baron,
Slicing through the lance shafts and the bucklers,
Through feet and fists, saddles and sides.
Anyone who had seen him dismembering Saracens,   1970

Piling up their bodies on the ground,
Would have remembered what a good vassal was.
Nor does he forget the battle-cry of Charles;
He shouts out 'Monjoie', loud and clear,
1975 Then calls to Roland, his friend and his peer:
'Lord companion, come and fight at my side.
In great sorrow we shall part this day.'   AOI.

148

Roland looks at Oliver's face;
It was colourless, livid, pale and wan.
1980 The clear red blood streams forth from his body
And splashes of it fall upon the ground.
'God,' said the count, 'I do not know what to do.
Lord companion, your courage has done you no good;
No man will ever be your equal.
1985 O, fair land of France, how bereft you will be today
Of good vassals, destroyed and ruined!
The emperor will suffer a grievous loss through this.'
With these words he faints upon his horse.   AOI.

149

See now Roland fainted upon his horse
1990 And Oliver, who has a mortal wound.
He has lost so much blood that his sight is blurred;
Neither near nor far can he see clearly enough
To be able to recognize a living soul.
His companion, when he encountered him,
1995 Receives a blow on his helmet studded with gold and gems.
He cleaves right through it down to the nasal,
But the blow did not reach as far as his head.
At this blow Roland looked at him
And asked him in gentle, tender tones:
2000 'Lord companion, do you intend to do this?
This is Roland who loves you so dearly;
You had not challenged me in any way.'

Oliver said: 'Now I can hear your voice,
But I cannot see you; may God watch over you.
Did I strike you? Pardon me for this.'   2005
Roland replies: 'I have not been hurt;
I pardon you here and before God.'
With these words they bowed to each other;
See how they part with such great love!

150
Oliver feels that he is in the grip of death.   2010
Both his eyes roll within his head;
His hearing and his vision are now completely gone.
He dismounts and lies down upon the ground;
He confesses his sins loud and clear
With both his hands joined and raised to heaven.   2015
He beseeches God to grant him paradise
And he blessed Charles and the fair land of France,
And his companion Roland above all men.
His heart fails him, his helmet slips forward;
His entire body falls to the ground.   2020
The count is dead, he can delay no longer.
Roland the brave weeps for him and mourns;
Never will you hear greater grief on earth.

151
Now Roland sees that his friend is dead,
Lying face down, his head on the ground.   2025
He began to mourn him in tender fashion:
'Lord companion, how sad that you were so bold;
We have been together for days and years.
You have caused me no harm and I have not wronged you.
Now that you are dead, it grieves me to remain alive.'   2030
With these words the marquis faints
Upon his horse named Veillantif.
He is secure in his stirrups of pure gold;
Whichever way he leans, he cannot fall.

152

2035 Before Roland has regained consciousness,
Recovered from his faint or come round,
Grievous losses have been sustained by his men.
The Franks are dead, he has lost every single one,
Except for the archbishop and Gautier del Hum,
2040 Who has come back down from the mountains.
He has fought valiantly against the men of Spain;
His men are dead, vanquished by the pagans.
Whether he likes it or not, he flees through the valleys
And calls out for Roland's help:
2045 'O, noble count, valiant man, where are you?
Never did I know fear when you were there.
This is Gautier who conquered Maelgut,
The nephew of Droun, the old and the hoary.
My courage used to make me your favourite.
2050 My lance shaft is broken and my shield pierced
And the mail of my hauberk is shattered and rent.
I have been wounded in the body by the thrust of a lance;
I shall soon die, but I have sold my life dearly.'
As he spoke thus, Roland heard him;
2055 He spurs on his horse and comes galloping towards him.   AOI.

153

Roland is full of grief and overcome with rage.
In the great throng he begins to strike,
Throwing twenty men from Spain down dead.
Gautier did the same for six and the archbishop five.
2060 The pagans say: 'These men are villains;
Mind, lords, that they do not escape alive.
A curse on the man who does not attack them
And a coward is he who allows them to escape!'
Then once more they raise the hue and cry
2065 And from all sides renew the attack.   AOI.

154

Count Roland was a noble warrior
And Gautier del Hum is a very fine knight,
The archbishop a worthy man of well-tried valour.
They have no wish to desert each other.
In the great throng they strike at the pagans;   2070
A thousand Saracens dismount
And forty thousand remain on horseback.
But, I believe, they dare not close in;
They hurl lances and spears at them,
Wigars and darts . . .   2075
And pikes, javelins and shafts.*   2075a
With the first volley they killed Gautier
And pierced the shield of Turpin of Reims;
Breaking his helmet and wounding him in the head.
They smashed and tore the mail in his hauberk
And wounded him in the body with four spears.   2080
Beneath him they kill his war-horse;
There is great sorrow, when the archbishop falls.   AOI.

155

When Turpin of Reims feels himself struck down,
Pierced through the body by four spears,
He quickly jumped to his feet.   2085
He looks at Roland, then ran towards him
And spoke these words: 'I am not vanquished;
A good vassal will never give up whilst still alive.'
He draws Almace, his sword of burnished steel;
In the great throng he strikes a thousand blows and more.   2090
Later Charles said that he did not spare a single one.
Around him Charles finds some four hundred men,
Some wounded, some pierced right through,
Some of them with their heads cut off.
So say the annals and the man who was on the field,   2095
The noble Giles, for whom God performs miracles.
He wrote the charter in the church of Laon.
He who does not know as much has not properly understood.

156

Count Roland fights on nobly;
2100 But his body is very hot and bathed in sweat.
In his head he feels pain and a great ache;
His temples are burst from the blowing of the horn.
But he wants to know if Charles will come;
He draws forth the oliphant and gave a feeble blow.
2105 The emperor halted and listened to him:
'Lords,' he said, 'things are going very badly for us;
Roland, my nephew, will be lost to us this day.
From the sound of the horn I can tell he has not long;
Let those who want to reach him ride fast!
2110 Blow your bugles, as many as there are in this army.'
Sixty thousand men blow so loudly
That the mountains ring out and the valleys respond.
The pagans hear them and they did not take it lightly.
They say to each other: 'We shall soon have Charles here.'

157

2115 The pagans say: 'The emperor is returning.   AOI.
Hear how the men of France sound their bugles;
If Charles comes, we shall have great losses.
Our war will begin afresh, if Roland is alive;
We have lost Spain, our land.'
2120 Some four hundred assemble, their helmets laced,
And they think themselves to be the finest on the field.
They attack Roland violently and savagely;
Now the count is under great pressure.   AOI.

158

When Count Roland sees them approach,
2125 He becomes so strong, so fierce, so alert.
As long as he remains alive, he will not yield to them;
He sits astride his horse named Veillantif
And urges it on well with his spurs of pure gold.
In the great throng he carries the attack to them

And Archbishop Turpin joins with him.   2130
One pagan said to the next: 'Come on now, friend!
We have heard the bugles of the men of France;
Charles, the mighty king, is on his way back.'

159

Count Roland never loved a coward,
Nor arrogant men nor those of evil character,   2135
Nor any knight, unless he were a good vassal.
He called to Archbishop Turpin:
'Lord, you are on foot and I am on horseback;
For love of you I shall make a stand here.
Together we shall endure both good and ill;   2140
I shall not abandon you because of any man.
Before long we shall make the pagans pay for this assault;
The finest blows are those which come from Durendal.'
The archbishop said: 'A curse on him who does not strike well;
Charles, who will avenge us well, is on his way back.'   2145

160

The pagans say: 'How sad that we were ever born!
What a fateful day has dawned for us today!
We have lost our lords and our peers;
Charles, the brave, is returning with his great army.
We can hear the clear bugles of the men of France;   2150
The noise from the call of "Monjoie" is great.
Count Roland is a man of such great ferocity
That he will never be vanquished by mortal man.
Let us cast our spears at him and then leave him be.'
And this they did with darts and wigars in abundance,   2155
Spears and lances and feathered javelins.
Roland's shield was broken and pierced
And the mail in his hauberk smashed and torn.
They failed to get through to his body;
But Veillantif was wounded in thirty places.   2160
It was left for dead beneath the count's body.

The pagans take flight, leaving him be;
Count Roland remains there on foot. AOI.

161

The pagans flee, angry and wrathful,
2165 Returning towards Spain with all haste.
Count Roland has no way of pursuing them;
He has lost his war-horse, Veillantif.
Like it or no, he remains on foot.
He went to help Archbishop Turpin
2170 And unlaced his golden helmet from his head.
He removed his light and shining hauberk
And cut his tunic into strips.
He placed the pieces in his great wounds
And then drew him to his breast in close embrace;
2175 Afterwards he laid him down gently on the green grass.
He beseeched him with great tenderness:
'O, noble man, pray give me leave to go;
Our companions, whom we loved so dearly,
Are now all dead; we must not leave them there.
2180 I intend to go and look for them and pick them out
And place them here before you, side by side.'
The archbishop said: 'Leave and then return;
This is your field and mine, thanks be to God.'

162

Roland sets off across the field alone;
2185 He searches the valleys and he searches the mountains.
There he found Gerin and Gerer, his companion,
And he found Berenger and Atton;
There he found Anseis and Samson
And he found Gerard of Roussillon, the old.
2190 One by one the brave man fetched them all;
He brought them right up to the archbishop
And placed them in a row before his knees.
The archbishop cannot hold back his tears;

He raises his hand, gives his blessing,
Then said: 'What a fate has befallen you, lords!   2195
May God, the Glorious One, receive all your souls;
May He place them amongst celestial flowers.
My own death fills me with such anguish;
Never again shall I see the mighty emperor.'

163

Roland sets off to scour the field.   2200
He found his companion Oliver
And, clasping him tightly to his breast,
Comes, as best he can, to the archbishop.
He laid him on a shield with the others
And the archbishop absolved them with the cross;   2205
Then his grief and pity grows more intense.
Roland says: 'Fair companion Oliver,
You were the son of Duke Renier,
Who held the march of the Vale of Runers.
For breaking shafts and shattering shields,   2210
For vanquishing and dismaying the arrogant,
For sustaining and counselling worthy men,
And vanquishing and dismaying miscreants,
In no land is there a finer knight.'

164

When Count Roland sees his peers dead   2215
And Oliver, whom he loved so dearly,
He was filled with emotion and begins to weep;
The colour drained completely from his face.
So great was his grief that he could not remain standing;
Like it or no, he falls to the ground in a faint.   2220
The archbishop said: 'What an unhappy fate, baron!'

165

When the archbishop saw Roland swoon,
He suffered more grief than he had ever known;
He stretched forth his hand and took the oliphant.

2225 At Rencesvals there is a running stream;
He wants to reach it and give Roland some water from it.
With faltering steps he makes his way towards it;
So weak is he that he can go no further.
Having lost so much blood, he lacks the strength.
2230 In less time than it takes to cover a single acre,
His heart fails and he toppled forward;
A painful death is now upon him.

166

Count Roland recovers from his faint;
He rises to his feet, but his agony is great.
2235 He looks uphill and he looks downhill;
On the green grass beyond his companions
He perceives the noble baron lying there;
It is the archbishop, sent by God to be his servant;
He confesses his sins and looks upwards;
2240 He joined both his hands and raised them heavenwards,
Beseeching God to grant him paradise.
Turpin, Charles's warrior, is dead;
In great battles and with very fine sermons
Against the pagans he was a constant champion.
2245 May God grant him his holy blessing.   AOI.

167

Count Roland sees the archbishop on the ground;
He sees his entrails spilled and lying around his body.
Beneath his brow his brains flow forth;
Upon his chest, across the breast,
2250 He crossed his fine, white hands.
He mourns him out loud, in the fashion of his land:
'O, noble man, knight of high birth,
This day I entrust you to the Glorious One in heaven.
Never will any man serve him more willingly;
2255 Since the apostles there was never such a prophet
For maintaining the faith and winning men over.

May your soul know no suffering
And find the gate of paradise wide open.'

168
Roland feels that his death is near;
Through his ears his brains are seeping.   2260
He beseeches God to summon all his peers
And then prays on his own behalf to the angel Gabriel.
To prevent any reproach he took the oliphant
And seized Durendal in his other hand.
Further than a crossbow can fire an arrow   2265
He goes over towards Spain, into a fallow field;
He climbs on to a mound, beneath a beautiful tree.
Four great marble blocks are there
And on the green grass he fell upon his back.
There he fainted, for death is close to him.   2270

169
High are the hills and the trees tower up;
There are four great blocks of shining marble.
Count Roland faints on the green grass;
A Saracen watches him all the while,
Feigning death and lying amongst the others.   2275
He has smeared his body and his face with blood;
He gets to his feet and rushes forward.
He was handsome and strong and very brave;
In his arrogance he embarks on an act of mortal folly.
He seized Roland's body and his armour   2280
And spoke thus: 'Charles's nephew is vanquished.
I shall take this sword to Arabia.'
As he drew it out, the count began to come round.

170
Roland senses that he is taking away his sword;
He opened his eyes and spoke these words to him: 2285
'You are not one of our men, it seems to me.'

He grasps the oliphant, which he never wanted to lose,
And strikes him on his golden helmet, studded with gold and
    gems.
He shatters the steel, his skull and his bones;
2290 He put both his eyes out of their sockets
And cast him down dead at his feet.
Then he says: 'Wretched pagan, how did you dare
Grab hold of me, without thought for right or wrong?
Anyone who hears of this will regard you as mad.
2295 Now my oliphant is split at its broad end;
The crystal and the gold have come away.'

171

Roland feels that he has lost his sight;
He rises to his feet, exerting all his strength.
All the colour has drained from his face.
2300 Before him lies a dark-hued stone;
On it he strikes ten blows in sorrow and bitterness.
The steel grates, but does not break or become notched;
'O, Holy Mary,' said the count, 'help me!
O, my good sword Durendal, what a fate you have suffered!
2305 Now that I am dying, I have no more need of you;
With you I have won so many battles in the field
And conquered so many vast lands,
Which Charles with the hoary-white beard now holds.
May you never be owned by a man who flees in battle!
2310 A very fine vassal has held you for so long;
There will never be such a man in blessed France.'

172

Roland struck the sardonyx stone;
The steel grates, but does not shatter or become notched.
When he saw that he could not break it,
2315 He begins to lament over it to himself:
'O, Durendal, how fair and clear and white you are!
How you shimmer and sparkle in the sun!

Charles was in the Vales of Maurienne,
When through his angel God on high told him
To give you to a captain count.   2320
Then the noble and mighty king girded it on me.
With it I conquered Anjou and Brittany
And with it I conquered Poitou and Maine;
With it I conquered Normandy the free
And with it I conquered Provence and Aquitaine   2325
And Lombardy and all Romagna.
With it I conquered Bavaria and all Flanders
And Burgundy and all Apulia.
And Constantinople, which rendered homage to him.
In Saxony his commands are obeyed.   2330
With it I conquered Scotland and Ireland
And England, which became his domain;
With it I have conquered so many lands and countries
Which Charles with the white beard now holds.
For this sword I grieve and sorrow;   2335
I should rather die than leave it in pagan hands.
God, our Father, spare France this disgrace!'

173
Roland struck upon the dark-hued stone;
He hacks away more of it than I can tell.
The sword grates, but neither breaks nor shatters;   2340
It rebounds towards heaven.
When the count sees that he cannot break it,
He lamented over it to himself very softly:
'O, Durendal, how fair and sacred you are!
In the golden hilt there are many relics: 2345
Saint Peter's tooth and some of Saint Basil's blood;
Some hair from the head of my lord Saint Denis
And part of the raiment of the Blessed Virgin.
It is not right for pagans to possess you;
You must be wielded by Christians.   2350
May no coward ever have you!
With you I have conquered vast lands.

103

Charles with the hoary-white beard now holds them;
They have made the emperor mighty and rich.'

174

2355 Roland feels that death is upon him;
It is moving down from his head to his heart.
He ran over to a pine and beneath it
And lay face down on the green grass.
He places his sword and the oliphant beneath him;
2360 Towards the pagan host he turned his head,
Because it was his earnest wish that
Charles and all his men should say
That he, the noble count, had died victoriously.
He confesses his sins over and over again;
2365 For his sins he proffered his glove to God.   AOI.

175

Roland feels that his time has come;
He is on a steep hill facing Spain.
With one hand he beat his breast:
'O God, the Almighty, I confess
2370 My sins, both great and small,
Which I have committed since the time I was born,
Until this day on which I have been overtaken.'
He held out his right glove to God;
Angels come down to him from Heaven.   AOI.

176

2375 Count Roland lay down beneath a pine tree;
He has turned his face towards Spain.
Many things began to pass through his mind:
All the lands which he conquered as a warrior,
The fair land of France, the men of his lineage,
2380 Charlemagne, his lord, who raised him.
He cannot help weeping and heaving great sighs;
But he does not wish to be unmindful of himself.

He confesses his sins and prays for the grace of God:
'True Father, who has never lied,
You who brought back Lazarus from the dead   2385
And rescued Daniel from the lions,
Protect my soul from every peril
And from the sins which I have committed in my life.'
He proffered his right glove to God;
Saint Gabriel took it from his hand.   2390
Roland laid his head down over his arm;
With his hands joined he went to his end.
God sent down his angel Cherubin
And with him Saint Michael of the Peril.
With them both came Saint Gabriel.   2395
They bear the count's soul to paradise.

177
Roland is dead, God has his soul in heaven.
The emperor arrives at Rencesvals;
There is no road or path there,
No open space, no yard or foot,   2400
Not covered with either Franks or pagans.
Charles cries out: 'Where are you, fair nephew?
Where is the archbishop and Count Oliver?
Where is Gerin and his companion Gerer?
Where is Oton and Count Berenger,   2405
Yvon and Yvoire, whom I loved so dearly?
What has become of the Gascon Engeler,
Duke Samson and Anseis the brave?
Where is Gerard of Roussillon, the old,
And the twelve peers whom I had left behind?'   2410
To what avail, when no one could reply?
'O God,' said the king, 'what great sorrow
That I was not here when battle commenced.'
He tugs at his beard like a man beset with grief;
His brave knights shed tears.   2415
Twenty thousand fall to the ground in a faint;
Duke Naimes feels very great pity.

178

There is no knight or baron there
Who does not weep copious tears of pity.
2420 They bewail their sons, their brothers, their nephews,
Their friends and their liege lords;
Many of them fall to the ground in a faint.
Duke Naimes then acted in a most worthy fashion;
He was first to speak to the emperor:
2425 'Look ahead, two leagues away from here
You can see, from the dust rising off the great highways,
That there are a great many pagans.
Ride on, avenge this sorrow!'
'O God,' said Charles, 'how very far away they are.
2430 Let justice and honour prevail;
They have robbed me of the flower of fair France.'
The king gives orders to Geboin and Oton,
Tedbald of Reims and Count Milon:
'Guard the battlefield, the valleys and the hills;
2435 Let the dead lie just as they are,
Without being touched by any lion or other beast.
Do not let them be touched by squire or servant;
I forbid you to let any man touch them,
Until God wishes us to return to this field.'
2440 And they reply with love and tenderness:
'Rightful emperor, dear lord, we shall do this.'
They retain a thousand of their men.   AOI.

179

The emperor has his bugles sounded;
Then he rides off with his great army.
2445 The men of Spain have turned their backs on them;
The Franks join together in close pursuit.
When the king sees the onset of evening,
He dismounts in a meadow, on the green grass,
Lies down on the ground and prays to God
2450 That for him he should stop the sun in its tracks,
Postpone nightfall and maintain daylight.

See, an angel now comes again and speaks to him;
Immediately he commanded the king:
'Charles, ride on, daylight will not fail you.
You have, as God knows, lost the flower of France;   2455
You can avenge yourself on this criminal race.'
With these words the emperor mounted his horse.   AOI.

180

God performed a great miracle for Charlemagne,
For the sun remained where it was.
The pagans are fleeing, the Franks are in close pursuit.   2460
In the Val Tenebros they catch up with them
And drive them on towards Saragossa with their blows.
Striking powerfully they keep on killing them;
They cut off their paths and their escape routes.
Before them now is the River Ebro;   2465
It is very deep, awesome and rapid.
There is no barge, dromond or lighter there;
The pagans call on one of their gods, Tervagant,
Then jump in, but they have no one to save them.
Those who are fully armed weigh most;   2470
Some of them sank straight to the bottom,
The others go floating downstream.
Those who survived longest swallowed so much water
That they were all drowned in dreadful pain.
The Franks shout: 'What a sad fate was yours, Roland!'   AOI.   2475

181

When Charles sees that all the pagans are dead,
Some slain and even more drowned,
His knights enjoy great booty,
The noble king has got down off his horse;
He prostrates himself on the ground and gave thanks to God.   2480
When he rises to his feet, the sun has set.
The emperor said: 'It is time to make camp;
It is too late to return to Rencesvals.

Our horses are weary and exhausted;
2485 Take off their saddles and the bridles from their heads
And let them graze in these meadows.'
The Franks reply: 'Lord, you speak wisely.'   AOI.

182

The emperor has pitched camp;
In the deserted land the Franks dismount.
2490 They removed the saddles from their horses
And they take down the golden bridles from their heads,
Turning them loose in the fresh grass of the meadows;
They cannot provide them with any other fodder.
Anyone overcome with fatigue sleeps on the ground;
2495 That night no one ever mounts guard.

183

The emperor has lain down in a meadow;
He places his great spear by his head.
That night he would not remove his armour,
And he wore his shining, saffron hauberk.
2500 He kept laced upon him his helmet studded with gold and gems
And girt about him his sword Joiuse, which had no peer
And whose colour changes thirty times a day.
We could speak for a long time about the lance
With which our Lord was wounded on the cross.
2505 Charles has its point, thanks be to God,
Which he has had mounted in his golden pommel.
Through this honour and this excellence
The name Joiuse was given to the sword.
Frankish barons should not forget it;
2510 From it they derive their battle cry 'Monjoie'.
For this reason no race on earth can withstand them.

184

The night is clear and the moon bright.
Charles lies down, but he is full of grief for Roland
And Oliver's fate distresses him deeply,
And also that of the twelve peers and the Frankish army.   2515
At Rencesvals he has left men dead and covered in blood;
He cannot prevent himself from weeping and mourning them
And he prays to God to protect their souls.
The king is weary, for his pain is very great.
He fell asleep, unable to do anything more;   2520
Throughout all the meadows the Franks lie asleep.
Not a single horse can remain standing;
Those which need grass eat it lying down.
He who knows true pain has learned a great deal.

185

Charles sleeps like a weary man.   2525
God sent Saint Gabriel to him;
He gives him orders to guard the emperor.
The angel spends all night at his head;
In a vision he announced to him
A battle to be waged against him   2530
And showed him its grim significance.
Charles looked up towards the sky;
He sees the thunderbolts, the winds and the frosts,
The storms and the terrible tempests,
And before his eyes appeared fire and flames,   2535
Which suddenly come tearing down on all his men,
Burning their shafts of ash and apple wood
And their shields, right up to their bosses of pure gold,
And splitting the shafts of their sharp spears.
Their hauberks and steel helmets grate.   2540
He sees his knights in great pain;
Then bears and leopards attempt to devour them,
Serpents, vipers, dragons and devils.
There are griffins there, more than thirty thousand;
They all swoop down on the Franks   2545

Who cry out: 'Charlemagne, help!'
The king feels great anguish and pity.
He tries to help them, but feels some restraint.
From a clearing a huge lion approaches;
2550 It was most terrible, hostile and fearsome.
It attacks and makes for his own person
And the two of them engage in a struggle.
But he cannot tell which strikes and which falls.
The emperor remains asleep.

186

2555 After this comes another vision:
That he was in France, at Aix, before a block of stone.
A bear cub was being held there by two chains;
From the Ardennes he could see thirty bears coming,
Each one of them speaking like a man.
2560 They said to him: 'Lord, give him back to us;
It is not right for him to remain any longer with you.
We must come to the help of our kinsman.'
From his palace a hunting dog comes running;
It attacked the largest of them
2565 On the green grass, beyond his companions.
The king witnessed such a terrible struggle,
But he does not know which one is winning and which not.
The angel of God showed all this to him;
Charles sleeps on until morning, at daybreak.

187

2570 King Marsile takes flight to Saragossa;
He dismounts in the shade, beneath an olive tree.
He lays down his sword, his shield and his byrnie;
On the green grass he lies down, a wretched sight.
He has lost his entire right hand;
2575 The blood flowing from it causes him to faint with pain.
Before him is his wife Bramimonde;
She weeps and wails, lamenting loudly.

With her are more than twenty thousand men
And they curse Charles and fair France.
They rush off to Apollo in a crypt,   2580
Rail against him and hurl abuse at him:
'O, wretched god, why do you cause us such shame?
Why did you permit our king to be destroyed?
Anyone who serves you well receives a poor reward.'
Then they grab his sceptre and his crown   2585
And hang him by his hands from a pillar;
Then they send him flying to the ground at their feet
And beat him and smash him to pieces with huge sticks.
They seize Tervagant's carbuncle
And fling Muhammad into a ditch   2590
Where pigs and dogs bite and trample on him.

188

Marsile has regained consciousness.
He has himself carried into his vaulted bedchamber;
Many colours are depicted and portrayed there
And Bramimonde, the queen, weeps for him.   2595
She tears at her hair and bewails her fate;
Thereupon she cries out at the top of her voice:
'O, Saragossa, how you have been deprived this day
Of the noble king who held you in his power!
Our gods committed a grave crime   2600
In failing him this morning in battle.
The emir will turn out to be a coward,
If he does not fight these bold men,
Who are so fierce that they disregard their own lives.
The emperor with the hoary-white beard   2605
Is full of valour and great daring.
If there is a battle, he will never take flight;
It is a great pity that there is no one to kill him.'

189

The emperor in his great power
2610 Has been in Spain for seven long years;
There he captures castles and a number of cities.
King Marsile does what is necessary;
In the first year he had his letters sealed
And sent word to Baligant in Babylon –
2615 He is the old emir, a man of great age,
Who has outlived both Virgil and Homer –
To come to his aid in Saragossa.
If he fails to do so, he would abandon his gods
And all his idols, which it is his custom to adore,
2620 And receive holy Christianity;
He would be willing to make peace with Charlemagne.
Baligant is far away and he took his time;
He summons his men from forty kingdoms,
And prepared his great dromonds,
2625 Warships, barges, galleys and boats.
Below Alexandria there is a seaport;
There he made ready his entire fleet.
Then in May, on the first day of summer;
He set sail with all his forces.

190

2630 Vast are the forces of this infidel race;
They sail rapidly, rowing and steering.
At the mastheads and on the lofty prows
There are many carbuncles and lanterns;
From up on high they cast so much light
2635 That by night the sea becomes more beautiful,
And, when they arrive at the land of Spain,
The whole country is lit up and illuminated by them.
The news of this reaches Marsile.   AOI.

191

The pagan forces would not delay;
2640 They leave the sea and enter fresh water.
They pass by Marbrise and by Marbrose;

All the ships head up the River Ebro.
There are many lanterns and carbuncles on them,
Which all night long provide much light;
That day they arrive at Saragossa.   AOI.   2645

192

The day is clear and the sun shines brightly;
The emir disembarked from the lighter.
On the right Espaneliz accompanies him
And seventeen kings follow on behind;
I cannot tell how many dukes and counts are there.   2650
Beneath a laurel tree, which stands in a field,
They fling down on the green grass a white silk cloth;
And there placed an ivory throne.
On it sits the pagan Baligant;
All the others remain standing.   2655
Their lord was first to speak:
'Listen now, noble and valiant knights;
Charles the king, the emperor of the Franks,
Must not eat, unless I say the word.
Throughout all Spain he has waged a mighty war on me;   2660
I intend to pursue him in the fair land of France.
I shall not rest for the remainder of my life,
Until he is dead or has surrendered still alive.'
He strikes his right gauntlet against his knee.

193

When he had spoken thus, he made a firm resolve   2665
That all the gold on earth would not prevent him
From going to Aix where Charles holds his court.
His men advise him and gave him counsel;
Then he summoned two of his knights,
One of them is Clarifan, the other Clarien: 2670
'You are sons of King Maltraien
Who used to act as my willing messenger.
I bid you to go to Saragossa

And on my behalf inform Marsile
2675 That I have come with help against the Franks.
If I find the right place, there will be a great battle;
And give him this folded gauntlet edged with gold;
Have him put it on his right hand
And take him this rod of pure gold
2680 And let him come to pay homage to me for his fief.
I shall go to France to wage war against Charles;
If he does not kneel at my feet, at my mercy,
And should he refuse to forsake the Christian faith,
I shall seize the crown from his head.'
2685 The pagans reply: 'Lord, you speak most wisely.'

194

Baligant said: 'Ride onwards, barons;
Let one carry the glove, the other the staff.'
And they reply: 'Dear lord, we shall do it.'
They rode on until they reach Saragossa;
2690 They pass through ten gates, cross four bridges
And travel along all the streets where the burgesses live.
As they approach the city up above,
They heard a commotion from the direction of the palace.
There are many of the pagans there,
2695 Weeping and wailing, displaying great sorrow;
They mourn their gods, Tervágant and Muhammad
And Apollo, which they have no longer.
They say to each other: 'Unhappy ones, what will become of us?
Utter disaster has befallen us.
2700 We have lost King Marsile;
Yesterday Count Roland sliced off his right hand.
We no longer have Jurfaleu the Blond;
The whole of Spain will today be at their mercy.'
The two messengers get off their horse at the block.

195

They leave their horses beneath an olive tree;   2705
Two Saracens took them by the reins
And the messengers held each other by their cloaks.
Then they went up to the palace on high.
When they entered the vaulted chamber,
As a mark of friendship they made an unfortunate greeting: 2710
'May Muhammad, who has us in his power,
And Tervagant and Apollo, our lord,
Save the king and protect the queen.'
Bramimonde said: 'Now I hear great foolishness.
These gods of ours have abandoned the fight;   2715
At Rencesvals their powers deserted them;
They allowed our knights to be slain
And they let down my own lord in battle.
He has lost his right hand, he no longer has it;
Count Roland the powerful cut it off.   2720
Charles will have the whole of Spain in his power;
What will become of me, miserable wretch?
O, woe is me that I have no one to kill me.'   AOI.

196

Clarien said: 'My lady, do not say such things;
We are messengers from the pagan Baligant.   2725
He will be Marsile's protector, he says,
And he sends him his staff and his gauntlet.
We have four thousand lighters on the Ebro,
Warships and barges and swift galleys;
There are dromonds, more than I can say.   2730
The emir is rich and powerful;
He will pursue Charlemagne into France.
He intends to bring about his death or his surrender.'
Bramimonde said: 'He need not go so far!
You will find the Franks closer to where we are;   2735
He has now been in this land for seven years.
The emperor is valiant and a fine warrior;
He would sooner die than abandon the field.

No king on earth would regard him as a child.
2740   Charles fears no man alive.'

197

'That is enough,' said King Marsile.
He said to the messengers: 'Lords, speak to me.
You see now that I am in the grip of death;
I have no son or daughter or heir.
2745   I did have one, but he was killed last evening;
Tell my lord that he should come to see me.
The emir has rights in Spain;
If he wishes to have it, I renounce all rights over it.
Let him then defend it against the Franks.
2750   As for Charlemagne, I shall give him good advice;
He will have vanquished him within a month from now.
You can take him the keys of Saragossa;
Then tell him not to depart, if he trusts me.'
They reply: 'Lord, you speak truly.'   AOI.

198

2755   Marsile said: 'Charles the emperor
Has slain my men, laid waste my land
And shattered and ravaged my cities.
Last night he lay by the River Ebro;
I reckoned that he is no more than seven leagues away.
2760   Tell the emir to take his army there;
Through you I inform him, let battle be joined there.'
He handed over to him the keys of Saragossa.
The messengers both bowed low before him;
They take their leave and thereupon departed.

199

2765   The two messengers mounted their horses;
They swiftly leave the city.
Deeply disturbed they make their way to the emir

And present him with the keys of Saragossa.
Baligant said: 'What did you find?
Where is Marsile whom I had summoned?'   2770
Clarien said: 'He has a mortal wound.
Yesterday the emperor was going through the pass,
Intending to return to the fair land of France.
He had arranged a rearguard with great renown;
Count Roland, his nephew, was left behind in it,   2775
And Oliver and all the twelve peers,
And twenty thousand armed men from France.
King Marsile, the brave, joined battle with them;
He and Roland came face to face on the battlefield.
Roland gave him such a blow with Durendal   2780
That he severed his right hand from his body;
He killed his son whom he loved so much
And the men whom he had brought with him.
Unable to remain any longer, he took flight;
The emperor pursued him hotly.   2785
The king asks that you come to his aid;
He surrenders to you the kingdom of Spain.'
And Baligant begins to ponder;
His grief is so great that he almost went mad.   AOI.

                            200
'Lord emir,' said Clarien,   2790
'Yesterday a battle was fought at Rencesvals;
Roland died and Count Oliver as well,
And the twelve peers whom Charles loved so dearly.
Twenty thousand of their Franks died;
King Marsile lost his right arm   2795
And the emperor pursued him hotly.
There was no knight left in this land
Who was not slain or drowned in the Ebro.
The Franks are camped on the river bank;
They have come so close to us in this country   2800
That, if you wish it, withdrawal will be difficult for them.'
A fierce look comes over Baligant's face;

In his heart he is joyous and jubilant.
He rises to his feet from his throne,
2805 Then cries out: 'Barons, lose no time,
Leave your ships, mount your horses and ride.
If Charlemagne the old does not take flight now,
King Marsile will be avenged before the day is out.
For his right arm I shall present him with a head.'

201

2810 The pagans from Arabia left their ships,
Then they mounted their horses and their mules
And rode away, what else could they do?
The emir, who set them on their way,
Calls to Gemalfin, a trusted adviser:
2815 'I confer on you the task of assembling my host.'
Then he mounted his brown war-horse,
Taking four dukes along with him,
And he rode until he reached Saragossa.
He got off his horse at a marble block
2820 And four counts held his stirrup for him.
He climbs up the steps to the palace
And Bramimonde comes running to meet him.
She said to him: 'What an unhappy fate is mine!
I have lost my husband, lord, with such shame.'
2825 She falls at his feet and the emir raised her up;
Filled with grief, they came up into the chamber.   AOI.

202

When he sees Baligant, King Marsile
Then called to two Spanish Saracens:
'Take my arms and help me to sit up.'
2830 With his left hand he took one of his gauntlets.
Marsile said: 'Lord king, emir,
I hereby place all Spain in your hands*
And Saragossa and the fief which goes with it;
I have brought destruction upon myself and all my men.'

And he replies: 'So great is my grief   2835
That I cannot converse with you on this for long;
I am aware that Charles is not expecting me
And yet from you I accept this gauntlet.'
The grief he suffers caused him to depart in tears.   AOI.

203

He descends the palace steps,   2840
Mounts his horse and rides swiftly back towards his men.
He rode so fast that he soon outstrips them all.
Repeatedly he shouts out:
'Come on, pagans, for the Franks are already fleeing.'   AOI.

204

In the morning, at the first light of dawn,   2845
The emperor Charles awoke from his sleep.
Saint Gabriel, who watches over him on God's behalf,
Raises his hand and makes the sign of the cross over him.
The king rises and laid aside his armour;
And throughout the host the others disarm themselves;   2850
Then they mounted their horses and ride at top speed
Following the long roads and the broad highways.
They make their way to see the terrible destruction
At Rencesvals, where the battle took place.   AOI.

205

Charles has reached Rencesvals;   2855
The dead bodies he finds there bring tears to his eyes.
He said to the Franks: 'Lords, slow down.
For I myself must go out ahead
Because of my nephew, whom I would like to find.
Once I was at a solemn festival in Aix   2860
And my valiant knights boasted
Of great battles and violent struggles;
I heard Roland make a claim:

Never would he die on foreign soil
2865 Without advancing beyond his men and his peers.
His head would be turned towards the enemies' land,
And he would end his days as a conqueror.'
Further than one can cast a stick
Charles climbed a hill ahead of all the rest.

206

2870 When the emperor goes in search of his nephew,
He found in the meadow the flowers of so many plants,
Each stained red with the blood of our barons.
Beset with grief, he cannot hold back his tears.
Charles has arrived beneath two trees;
2875 He recognized Roland's blows on three blocks of stone.
He sees his nephew lying on the green grass;
It is no wonder that Charles is distressed.
He dismounts and made his way swiftly to where he lay;
He takes him in both hands
2880 And, such is his anguish, faints upon him.

207

The emperor came round from his faint.
Duke Naimes and Count Acelin,
Geoffrey of Anjou and his brother Thierry,
Take hold of the king, drawing him to his feet beneath a pine.
2885 He looks at the ground and sees his nephew lying there;
He began to mourn him so tenderly:
'Beloved Roland, may God have mercy on you!
No man has ever seen such a knight
For starting great battles and bringing them to an end.
2890 Now my fame has begun its decline.'
Charles faints, he could not prevent it.   AOI.

208

Charles the king came round from his faint;
Four of his barons hold him by the hands.
He looks down at the ground and sees his nephew lying there.
His body is robust, but drained of all its colour;   2895
His eyes are upturned and full of shadows.
Charles mourns him in faith and love:
'Beloved Roland, may God place your soul amidst the flowers
Of paradise, amongst the glorious ones.
How unfortunate was your coming to Spain, lord!*   2900
Never will a day dawn without my feeling sorrow for you.
How my strength and my ardour will decrease!
I shall never have anyone to sustain my honour;
I do not think I have a single friend on earth;
I may have kinsmen, but there is none so valiant.'   2905
He tears out handfuls of his hair;
A hundred thousand Franks feel such great grief
That there is not one who does not weep bitterly.   AOI.

209

'Beloved Roland, I shall return to France;
When I am in my chamber in Laon,   2910
Foreigners will come from many kingdoms.
They will ask: "Where is the captain count?"
I shall tell them he has died in Spain;
Henceforth I shall rule my kingdom with great distress.
No day will dawn without my weeping and lamenting.'   2915

210

'Beloved Roland, valiant man, noble youth,
When I am in my chapel in Aix,
My vassals will come and ask me for news.
The news I shall give will be terrible and cruel;
My nephew, who conquered so much for me, is dead.   2920
The Saxons will rise up against me,
And the Hungarians, Bulgars and so many heathen peoples,

Romans, Apulians and all those from Palermo
And Africans and those from Califerne:
2925 Then my troubles and my suffering will commence.
Who will lead my armies with such might,
Now that he is dead who has always been our captain?
O, fair land of France, how bereft you are!
My grief is so great that I no longer wish to live.'
2930 He begins to tear at his white beard;
With both hands he pulls the hair from his head.
A hundred thousand Franks fall to the ground in a faint.

211

'Beloved Roland, may God have mercy upon you;
May your soul be placed in paradise.
2935 He who killed you has brought destruction to France;
My grief is so great that I no longer wish to live,
Because of those in my household who died for me;
May God, the son of the Virgin Mary, grant that,
Before I reach the main pass of Cize,
2940 The soul be parted from my body this day,
Placed and set amidst theirs,
And may my flesh be buried next to theirs.'
His eyes stream with tears and he tugs at his white beard;
Duke Naimes said: 'Now Charles feels great sorrow.' AOI.

212

2945 'Emperor, lord,' said Geoffrey of Anjou,
'Do not display such bitter grief.
Search the entire field for our men
Whom the Spaniards have killed in battle;
Have them taken to a charnel-house.'
2950 The king said: 'For this purpose blow your horn.' AOI.

213

Geoffrey of Anjou blew his bugle;
The Franks dismount, Charles gave the order.
All their friends whom they found dead
Were taken at once to a charnel-house.
There are many bishops and abbots there,   2955
Monks, canons and tonsured priests,
And they absolved and signed them in God's name.
They had myrrh and thymiama kindled for them
And censed them all with great vigour.
They buried them with great honour;   2960
And then they left them; what else could they do?   AOI.

214

The emperor has Roland prepared for burial
And Oliver and Archbishop Turpin.
He had them all cut open before him
And all their hearts wrapped in silken cloth.   2965
They are placed in a white marble coffin
And then they took up the bodies of the barons.
They placed the lords in deerskins
And washed them in piment and in wine.
The king gives orders to Tedbald and Geboin,   2970
To Count Milon and Oton the marquis:
'Escort them in three carts along the highway.'
They are completely wrapped in oriental silk.   AOI.

215

The emperor Charles is set to depart,
When the vanguard of the pagans suddenly appears.   2975
Two messengers came from the ranks in front,
Announcing the impending battle in the emir's name:
'Arrogant king, it is not fitting for you to depart.
See how Baligant rides after you;
The armies he brings from Arabia are vast.   2980
This day we shall see if you possess true courage.'   AOI.

216

Charles the king took hold of his beard
And he recalls the sorrow and the destruction;
He looks fiercely at all his men,
2985   Then cries out in his loud, strong voice:
'Frankish barons, to horse and to arms!'   AOI.

217

The emperor is the first to arm himself;
He swiftly donned his byrnie.
He laces on his helmet and girt about him his sword Joiuse,
2990   Whose glitter is not diminished by the sun.
He hangs round his neck a shield from Viterbo,
Grasps his spear and brandishes its shaft.
Then he mounts Tencendur, his good horse –
He won it at the fords beneath Marsonne,
2995   Throwing Malpalin of Narbonne down dead from its back –
He gives it free rein and spurs it on repeatedly.
He springs forward, watched by a hundred thousand men,   AOI.
Calling on God and the pope in Rome.

218

Throughout the field the Franks dismount;
3000   More than a hundred thousand arm themselves together.
They have equipment which suits them perfectly,
Swift horses and very fine armour.
Then they mounted with great faith in their skill;
If they get the chance, they intend to give battle.
3005   Their pennons hang down over their helmets.
When Charles sees such fine countenances,
He called to Jozeran of Provence,
Duke Naimes and Antelme of Mayence:
'A man should have confidence in such vassals;
3010   He is a fool who bewails his fate in their company.
If the Arabs do not abandon their advance,
I intend to make them pay dearly for Roland's death.'
Duke Naimes replies: 'And may God grant us this.'   AOI.

219

Charles calls Rabel and Guineman.
The king said: 'Lords, I bid you   3015
Take the posts of Oliver and Roland.
Let one take the sword and the other the oliphant
And ride right out before us in the front,
With fifteen thousand Franks together with you,
From our finest and most valiant youths.   3020
After them there will be just as many
And Geboin and Lorant will lead them.'
Duke Naimes and Count Jozeran
Set about arranging these divisions.
If they get the chance, there will be a great battle.   AOI.   3025

220

The first two divisions are of Frenchmen;
After these two they draw up the third.
In this are the vassals from Bavaria;
They estimated it contained twenty thousand knights.
Never on their part will the battle be abandoned;   3030
There is no people on earth whom Charles loves more,
Apart from the men of France who conquered his realms for him.
Count Ogier the Dane, the warrior,
Will lead them, for this company is fierce.   AOI.

221

The emperor Charles has three divisions;   3035
Duke Naimes then drew up the fourth
From such barons as have great courage.
They are Germans and come from Germany;
There are twenty thousand of them, say all the others;
They are well equipped with horses and arms.   3040
Never for fear of death will they abandon a battle,
And Herman, the Duke of Thrace, will lead them.
He would sooner die there than become a coward.   AOI.

222

Duke Naimes and Count Jozeran
3045 Made up the fifth division with Normans;
They are twenty thousand, say all the Franks.
They have fine armour and good swift horses;
Never for fear of death will they concede defeat.
No people on earth are more effective on the field.
3050 Richard the Old will lead them in the field,
He will strike there with his sharp spear.   AOI.

223

They made up the sixth division of Bretons;
They have thirty thousand knights with them.
They ride their horses like true barons,
3055 With painted spear shafts and pennons fixed to them.
Their lord is called Oedun.
He gives orders to Count Nevelon,
To Tedbald of Reims and the Marquis Oton:
'Lead my men; I present you with this honour.'   AOI.

224

3060 The emperor now had six divisions made up,
Then Duke Naimes drew up the seventh
From Poitevins and barons from Auvergne:
There may be forty thousand knights in all.
They have good horses and most beautiful arms.
3065 They are by themselves in a valley beneath a hill,
And Charles blessed them with his right hand;
They will be led by Jozeran and Godselme.   AOI.

225

And the eighth division was drawn up by Naimes;
It is made up of Flemings and barons from Frisia.
3070 They have more than forty thousand knights;
Never will battle be abandoned on their part.

The king said: 'These men will serve me well.
Both Rembalt and Hamon of Galicia
Will lead them with true knightly valour.'   AOI.

226

Both Naimes and Count Jozeran   3075
Have made up the ninth division with valiant men,
Those from Lorraine and those from Burgundy.
They are fifty thousand in number,
With helmets laced on and clad in their byrnies;
They have strong spears with short shafts.   3080
If the Arabs do not delay their assault,
These men will strike them, if they offer battle.
Thierry will lead them, the Duke of Argonne.   AOI.

227

The tenth division is from the barons of France;
There are a hundred thousand of our best captains.   3085
They have robust bodies and fierce countenances;
Their hair is hoary, their beards are white,
And they are clad in hauberks and double-mailed byrnies.
They are girded with swords from France and Spain
And have fine shields with distinctive emblems;   3090
Then, having mounted their horses, they demand the battle.
They shout out 'Monjoie'; Charlemagne is with them.
Geoffrey of Anjou carries the oriflamme:
Saint Peter owned it and it was called Romaine;
But from Monjoie it has received a change in name.   AOI. 3095

228

The emperor gets down from his horse.
He prostrated himself on the green grass
And turns his face towards the rising sun
Calling on God most fervently:
'True father, defend me on this day,   3100

You who truly brought Jonah to safety,
From the whale which had him in its body,
And spared the King of Niniveh
And Daniel from the terrible torment,
3105 When he was caught inside the lions' den,
And the three children in a blazing fire.
May your love be with me this day;
In your mercy, if it pleases you, allow me
To gain revenge for my nephew, Roland.'

229

3110 Having said a prayer, he rises to his feet;
He signed himself with the all-powerful cross.
The king climbs on to his swift horse;
Naimes and Jozeran held the stirrup for him.
He takes his shield and his sharp spear;
3115 His body is noble, robust and comely,
His face is bright and he is of noble mien.
Then he rides off most resolutely;
They blow their bugles front and rear.
The oliphant boomed out above all the rest;
3120 The Franks shed tears of compassion for Roland.

230

The emperor rides on most nobly;
He positioned his beard over his byrnie.
Out of love for him the others do the same;
A hundred thousand Franks are thus recognizable.
3125 They pass by the hills and the loftiest rocks,
And the deep valleys and oppressive defiles.
They leave the passes and the waste land,
And made their way to the Spanish march,
Taking up their stand on a level plain.
3130 Baligant's advance troops return to him;
A Syrian gave his report:
'We have seen the arrogant King Charles,

His men are fierce, they have no thought of failing him.
Arm yourselves, you will soon have a battle.'
Baligant said: 'Now I hear tell of true valour;   3135
Blow your bugles so that my pagans know of this.'

231

Throughout the army they have their drums sounded,
And the trumpets and the bugles ring out loud and clear.
The pagans dismount to arm themselves;
The emir does not wish to delay,   3140
He dons a byrnie with its saffron skirts.
He laces on a helmet, studded with gold and gems,
Then at his left side he girds on his sword.
From his arrogance he gave it a name;
From that of Charles about which he had heard   3145
[He gave it the name of Preciuse]:*
That was his war-cry on the battlefield.
He had his knights utter this cry.
He hangs from his neck one of his large, broad shields;
Its boss is of gold and it is edged with crystal,   3150
Its neck strap is made from fine striped brocade.
He grasps his spear which is called Maltet,
Its shaft is as thick as any club.
The iron tip alone would make a mule fully laden.
Baligant mounted his war-horse,   3155
His stirrup was held by Marcule from Outremer;
His crotch is very large
And he has slender hips and broad ribs;
His chest is large and handsomely formed,
His shoulders are broad and his face is very fair,   3160
His look is fierce and his hair curly.
It was as white as a flower in summer;
His courage has often been tested in battle.
O God, what a noble baron, if only he were a Christian!
He spurs on his horse and from it spurts clear blood.   3165
He springs forward and leaps across a ditch
Which can be measured at fifty feet.

The pagans cry: 'This is a man to protect the marches;
There is no Frank who, if he joins battle with him,
3170 Will not lose his life, like it or not.
Charles is a fool not to have taken flight.'   AOI.

232

The emir has the look of a true baron;
His beard is white, just like a flower,
And he is very learned in his faith
3175 And fierce and arrogant in battle.
His son Malpramis is a very fine knight;
He is tall and strong and takes after his ancestors.
He said to his father: 'Lord, let us ride onwards;
It would surprise me if we ever saw Charles.'
3180 Baligant said: 'Yes we shall, for he is very brave.
There are reports in many annals of his honourable deeds;
But he no longer has Roland, his nephew;
He will lack the might to withstand us.'   AOI.

233

'Fair son Malpramis,' said Baligant to him,
3185 'The other day that fine vassal Roland was killed,
And Oliver, the brave and the valiant,
The twelve peers, whom Charles loved so dearly,
And twenty thousand of the Frankish warriors.
I have a very low opinion of the rest.'

234

3190 'It is certain that the emperor is on his way back,
My messenger, the Syrian, has informed me of this;
He has drawn up ten very large divisions.
The man who blows the oliphant is very brave;
His companion responds with a clear bugle call
3195 And these men ride in the vanguard,
Together with fifteen thousand Franks,

Youths whom Charles calls children.
After these there are others just as numerous;
They will strike most ferocious blows.'
Malpramis said: 'I ask you for the first blow.'   AOI.   3200

235

'My son Malpramis,' said Baligant to him,
'I grant you whatever you have asked of me here.
You will go at once to fight against the Franks,
And you will take Torleu, the Persian king, with you,
And Dapamort, another king, from Lycia.   3205
If you succeed in destroying this great arrogance,
I shall grant you a portion of my land,
From Cheriant as far as the Val Marchis.'
He replies: 'Lord, I thank you.'
He advances to receive the gift: 3210
It is the land which belonged to King Flori.
Never again was he to see it
And he was never to take possession of his fief.

236

The emir rides forth through the ranks;
His son, whose body is huge, follows him.   3215
King Torleu and King Dapamort
Quickly draw up thirty divisions.
They each have a mighty force of knights;
The smallest division had fifty thousand men.
The first is made up of men from Butentrot   3220
And the next of the large-headed Milceni;
On their spines, along the middle of their backs,
They are as bristly as pigs.   AOI.

237

The third is made up of Nubles and Blos,
The fourth of Bruns and Slavs,   3225
The fifth of Sorbres and Sors,

The sixth of Armenians and Moors
The seventh of men from Jericho,
The eighth of Nigres and the ninth of Gros
3230 And the tenth of men from Balide the Strong,
They are a people to whom good deeds are unknown.   AOI.

238
The emir swears as earnestly as he can
By the powers and the body of Muhammad:
'Charles of France rides like a madman,
3235 There will be a battle, if he does not withdraw;
Never again will he wear a golden crown on his head.'

239
Then they draw up ten more divisions.
The first is of ugly Canaanites;
They came across from Val Fuit.
3240 The next is of Turks and the third of Persians,
The fourth of the fiery Petchenegs,*
The fifth of Soltras and Avars,
The sixth of Ormaleus and Eugies,
The seventh of the people of Samuel,
3245 The eighth of Bruise, the ninth of Clavers
And the tenth of people from Occian the Desert;
They are a race which does not serve the Lord God.
You could never hear of more villainous men,
Their skins are as hard as iron.
3250 For this reason they scorn helmets and hauberks;
In battle they are treacherous and fiery.   AOI.

240
The emir forms ten more divisions.
The first is made up of the giants of Malprose,
The next of Huns and the third of Hungarians
3255 And the fourth of men from Baldise the Long

And the fifth of men from Val Penuse
And the sixth of those from Marose
And the seventh of Lechs and Astrimoines;
The eighth is from Argoille and the ninth from Clarbone
And the tenth contains the bearded men from Fronde.   3260
They are a people who never loved God.
The Frankish annals list thirty divisions there;
Vast are the armies in which the bugles sound.
The pagans ride forth like valiant men.   AOI.

241

The emir is a very powerful man;   3265
Before him he has his dragon standard carried
And the standards of Tervagant and Muhammad
And a statue of the treacherous Apollo.
Ten Canaanites ride about him;
They shout out these words at the top of their voice: 3270
'Let him who wants protection from our gods,
Pray to them and serve them with great humility.'
The pagans lower their heads and their chins;
They bow their shining helmets low.
The Franks say: 'You will soon die, villains;   3275
May today see you destroyed.
O God of ours, protect Charles!
Let this battle be waged in His name.'   AOI.

242

The emir is a man of great wisdom;
He calls his sons and the two kings to him: 3280
'Lord barons, you will ride in the forefront
And lead all my divisions;
But I wish to keep three of the finest:
One will be of Turks and the other of Ormaleus
And the third of the giants of Malprose.   3285
The men of Occian will ride together with me
And they will join battle with Charles and the Franks.

The emperor, if he clashes with me,
Cannot fail to lose the head from his body.
3290 Let him be certain, he will have no other right.'   AOI.

243

Vast are the armies and handsome the divisions;
There is no hill, vale or mound between them,
No forest or wood: there can be no hiding-place.
They see each other clearly on the plain.
3295 Baligant said: 'My infidels,
Ride on in search of battle.'
Amborre of Oluferne carries the standard;
The pagans shout out the name of Preciuse.
The Franks say: 'May you be destroyed this day!'
3300 Loud and clear they renew their cry of 'Monjoie';
The emperor has his bugles sounded there
And the oliphant which gives them great encouragement.
The pagans say: 'Charles has fine men;
We shall have a battle which is hard and cruel.'   AOI.

244

3305 Vast is the plain and broad the countryside;
The helmets glitter with their gold and precious stones
And the shields and saffron byrnies
And the spears with their ensigns attached.
The bugles sound, the notes are loud and clear;
3310 The oliphant peals out loudly.
The emir calls to his brother,
He is Canabeus, the King of Floredee;
He held the land as far as Val Sevree.
Baligant pointed out Charles's divisions to him:
3315 'See the pride of France the renowned!
The emperor rides forth most fiercely;
He is in the rear with his bearded men.
Over their byrnies they have cast their beards,
Which are as white as snow on ice.

They will strike with lance and sword.   3320
We shall have a hard and violent battle;
Never has anyone seen such an engagement.'
Further than one can throw a peeled rod
Has Baligant ridden ahead of his companies.
He spoke and addressed them thus: 3325
'Onward, pagans, for I am going to advance.'
He brandished the shaft of his spear,
Turning the point towards Charles.   AOI.

245

When Charlemagne saw the emir
And the dragon, the ensign and the standard –   3330
There is such a vast force of Arabs
That on all sides they have occupied the country,
Except for those areas held by the emperor himself –
The King of France shouts out loud and clear:
'Frankish barons, you are fine vassals,   3335
You have fought on so many battlefields.
See the pagans; they are villains and cowards;
Their entire faith is not worth a penny.
If they have a huge army, what matter, my lords?
Let anyone who does not wish to come with me depart!'   3340
Then he urges on his horse with his spurs
And Tencendur made four leaps for him.
The Franks say: 'This king is valiant;
Ride, baron, none of us will fail you.'

246

The day was clear and the sun bright.   3345
The armies are handsome and the companies vast;
The divisions in front have joined battle.
Count Rabel and Count Guineman
Let go the reins of their swift horses
And spur on with zeal; then the Franks charge forward   3350
And begin to strike with their sharp spears.   AOI.

247

Count Rabel is a bold knight;
He urges on his horse with his spurs of pure gold
And goes to strike Torleu, the Persian king;
3355 No shield or byrnie could withstand the blow;
He plunged his golden spear deep into his body,
Knocking him down dead over a small bush.
The Franks say: 'May the Lord God help us!
Charles is in the right, we must not fail him.'   AOI.

248

3360 And Guineman fights with a king from Lycia;
He breaks all his shield with its painted flowers.
Then he tore apart his byrnie
And plunged his entire ensign deep into his body,
Flinging him dead, whoever may weep or laugh.
3365 At this blow the Franks shout out:
'Strike, barons, do not delay!
Charles is in the right against these men . . .
God has allowed us to administer His judgement.'   AOI.

249

Malpramis sits astride a horse which is pure white;
3370 He charges into the throng of Franks,
Striking great blows again and again,
Often piling one body on top of another.
Baligant is the first to shout:
'My barons, I have nurtured you for a long time;
3375 Look at my son; he is attacking Charles,
Challenging so many men with his weapons.
I could ask for no better vassal than he;
Help him with your sharp spears.'
With these words the pagans gallop forward;
3380 They strike violent blows, the engagement is very fierce.
The battle is terrible and grievous;
Never before or since has there been one so violent.   AOI.

250

The armies are vast and the companies fierce;
All the divisions have joined battle
And the pagans strike formidable blows.   3385
O God, so many shafts were broken there,
So many shields shattered and byrnies torn apart!
You would have seen the ground there so strewn with bodies,
The grass on the field which is green and tender
. . . .   3390
The emir calls upon his household:
'Strike, barons, against the Christian race.'
The battle is very violent and hard;
Never before or since has there been such a ferocious fight.
No end will be granted until all are dead.*   AOI.   3395

251

The emir calls to his men:
'Strike, pagans, you came for no other purpose!
I shall give you noble and beautiful wives,
And I shall give you fiefs and honours and lands.'
The pagans respond: 'We must not fail in this.'   3400
With mighty blows they lose some of their spears;
More than a hundred thousand swords were drawn.
Behold the clash is grievous and cruel!
Anyone who wants to be amongst them sees a battle.   AOI.

252

The emperor calls upon his Franks;   3405
'Lord barons, I love you and I trust in you;
You have fought so many battles for me,
Conquered so many kingdoms and removed so many kings.
I am fully aware that I owe you a reward,
Paid by my own person, in lands and wealth.   3410
Avenge your sons, your brothers and your heirs,
Who died the other day at Rencesvals.
You well know that I am in the right against the pagans.'

The Franks reply: 'Lord, you speak truly.'
3415 He has twenty thousand men with him;
They pledge their faith to him uniformly.
They will not fail him for fear of death or hardship;
There is no one who does not employ his lance.
With their swords they strike forthwith;
3420 The battle is terrible and harsh. AOI.

253

And Malpramis rides through the battlefield;
He causes havoc amongst the men of France.
Duke Naimes looks at him fiercely;
He goes to strike him like a powerful man.
3425 He breaks the upper part of his shield
And tears the saffron off the two skirts of his hauberk.
He plunges the whole of his yellow ensign into his body,
Flinging him dead amidst seven hundred others.

254

King Canabeus, the brother of the emir,
3430 Urges on his horse keenly with his spurs.
He drew his sword with its crystal pommel
And strikes Naimes on his princely helmet.
He shatters half of it on one side
Slicing through five of the laces with his sword of steel;
3435 His hood is not worth a penny.
He slices through the coif right down to his flesh,
Knocking a piece of it on to the ground.
It was a mightly blow which stunned the duke;
He would immediately have fallen, had God not helped him.
3440 He put his arms round the neck of his horse;
If the pagan had just managed to renew his attack,
The noble vassal would immediately have been killed.
Charles of France arrived to help him. AOI.

255

Duke Naimes is in such agony
And the pagan hastens to strike him.   3445
Charles said to him: 'Wretch, you will regret that blow.'
He goes to strike him with great courage
And breaks his shield, shattering it against his heart;
He tears the ventail off his hauberk,
Flinging him dead; his saddle remains empty.   3450

256

Charlemagne the king is filled with sorrow,
When he sees Naimes wounded before him,
His clear blood flowing over the green grass.
The emperor said to him quietly:
'Fair lord Naimes, ride along with me;   3455
The wretch who harassed you is dead.
I have just plunged my spear into his body.'
The Duke replies: 'Lord, I trust you;
If I survive, you will have a great reward for this.'
Then they united in love and faith;   3460
Together with them are twenty thousand Franks.
Not one fails to strike or wield his sword.   AOI.

257

The emir rides on through the battlefield,
And goes to strike Count Guineman.
He shatters his shining shield against his heart   3465
And tears the skirts off his hauberk.
He severs the two sides of his ribs,
Flinging him dead from his swift horse.
Then he killed Geboin and Lorant,
And Richard the Old, the lord of the Normans.   3470
The pagans shout out: 'Preciuse is powerful;
Strike, barons, we have our protector.'   AOI.

258

If only you had seen the knights from Arabia,
The men of Occian, of Argoille and Bascle!
3475 They strike fine blows with their spears,
But the Franks have no intention of fleeing.
Many men die there on both sides;
The violent battle lasts until evening falls.
The Frankish barons suffer great losses;
3480 Before it is broken off, there will be sorrow.　　　AOI.

259

The Franks and the Arabs strike fine blows;
They smash their shafts and their furbished spears.
Anyone who had seen the ruined shields,
Heard the ring of metal on shining hauberks
3485 And the grating of swords on helmets,
And anyone who had seen these knights toppling,
Men howling, as they fall dead upon the ground,
Would have many sorrowful memories!
This battle is very hard to endure.
3490 The emir calls upon Apollo
And Tervagant and Muhammad as well:
'My lord gods, I have served you well;
I shall fashion all your images from pure gold.'　　　AOI.
. . . .
3495 Suddenly, Gemalfin, a trusted counsellor, appears before him;
He brings bad news and says to him:
'Baligant, lord, things are going badly for you today;
You have lost your son Malpramis
And Canabeus, your brother, is slain.
3500 Fortune favoured two of the Franks;
The emperor is one, I believe.
His body is large and he looks just like a marquis;
His beard is as white as a flower in April.'
The emir keeps his helmet bowed low
3505 And then he lowers his face.
His grief is so great that he thought he would die
And he called to Jangleu from Outremer.

260

The emir said: 'Jangleu, come forward.
You are valiant and a man of great wisdom;
I have always followed your advice.   3510
What is your opinion about the Arabs and the Franks?
Are we the ones who will win the day?'
And he replies: 'You will die, Baligant;
Your gods will never protect you.
Charles is fierce and his men are valiant,   3515
I have never seen such warriors.
But call upon the barons of Occian,
Turks and Enfruns, Arabs and Giants.
Whatever must be, do not delay it.'

261

The emir drew forth his beard,   3520
Which was as white as a hawthorn flower;
Come what may, he does not wish to hide.
He places a clear-sounding bugle to his lips
And blows it loudly, so that the pagans heard it.
His companies rally thoughout the field;   3525
Those from Occian bray and whinny,
Those from Argoille yelp like hounds.
They attack the Franks with such great daring,
That in their thickest ranks they break and part them.
At this attack they cast seven thousand down dead.   3530

262

Count Ogier was not one to show cowardice;
Never did a better vassal than he don a byrnie.
When he saw the Frankish divisions smashed,
He called to Thierry, the Duke of Argonne,
Geoffrey of Anjou and Count Jozeran.   3535
He addresses Charles in the fiercest terms:
'See how the pagans are killing your men!
May it never please God that you wear a crown,

141

If you do not strike now to avenge your shame.'
3540 No one utters a single word in reply.
They spur on with zeal, giving free rein to their horses,
And go to strike the pagans, wherever they encounter them.

263

Charlemagne the king strikes good blows,   AOI.
And so do Duke Naimes, Ogier the Dane
3545 And Geoffrey of Anjou, who held the ensign.
Lord Ogier the Dane is very valiant,
He spurs on his horse, letting it go at full speed,
And goes to strike the man who held the dragon,
Making Amborre come crashing to the ground before him
3550 With the dragon and the royal ensign.
Baligant sees his pennon fall
And Muhammad's standard checked.
The emir thereby begins to realize
That he is wrong and Charlemagne right.
3555 The pagans from Arabia remain still.*
The emperor calls upon his kinsmen:
'Tell me, barons, in God's name, if I shall have your aid.'
The Franks reply: 'You have no need to ask;
A curse on him who does not strike with all his might.'   AOI.

264

3560 The day passes and evening falls.
The Franks and the pagans strike with their swords;
Those who brought the armies together are valiant.
They did not forget their battle-cries;
The emir cried out 'Preciuse'
3565 And Charles 'Monjoie', his renowned battle-cry.
They recognize each other's loud, clear voices
And both met in the middle of the field.
They go to strike each other and dealt mighty blows
With their spears on their wheel-patterned shields.
3570 They shattered them beneath their broad bosses

And severed the skirts from their hauberks,
Without touching each other's bodies.
They break their girths and turned over their saddles;
The kings fall and tumbled to the ground.
Immediately they rose to their feet;   3575
Very courageously they drew their swords.
This combat will never be averted;
Without one man dead, it cannot come to an end.   AOI.

265

Charles of fair France is very valiant;
He does not fear or dread the emir.   3580
They display their bare swords
And deal each other mighty blows on their shields.
They split the leather and double frames of wood.
The nails fall out and the bosses are smashed,
Then, without protection, they strike on their byrnies;   3585
The sparks fly up from their shining helmets.
This combat can never come to an end,
Until one of the men admits his wrong.   AOI.

266

The emir said: 'Charles, give some thought
To deciding to repent of your actions towards me;   3590
You have slain my son, as I know full well.
Your challenge for my country is unjust;
Become my vassal, I will return it to you as a fief.
Come and serve me from here to the Orient.'
Charles replies: 'This seems great villainy to me;   3595
I must render to a pagan neither peace nor love.
Receive the faith which God presents to us,
Christianity, and then I shall always love you.
Then serve and believe in the Almighty King.'
Baligant said: 'These are evil words.'   3600
Then they renew the fighting with their girded swords.   AOI.

143

267

The emir is a man of great strength;
He strikes Charlemagne on his helmet of burnished steel.
He broke and split the helmet on his head
3605 And drives his sword into his thick, curly hair.
He hacks off a full palm's breadth and more of flesh;
In that spot his bone stands exposed.
Charles staggers and almost fell;
But God did not want him to be slain or vanquished.
3610 Saint Gabriel came back to his side
And asked him: 'Mighty king, what are you doing?'

268

When Charles heard the sacred voice of the angel,
He has no fear or dread of death;
Strength and awareness return to him.
3615 He strikes the emir with his sword from France;
He breaks his helmet glittering with gems,
Slicing through his head and spilling out his brains
And through his entire face as far as his white beard.
He flings him dead and he has no chance of recovery.
3620 He shouts out 'Monjoie', his distinctive cry.
Hearing this Duke Naimes arrived;
He seizes Tencendur and the mighty king remounted.
The pagans turn tail, God does not want them to remain.
Now the Franks have the opportunity they ask for.

269

3625 The pagans flee as the Lord God wishes it.
The Franks give chase together with the emperor.
The king said: 'Lords, avenge your sorrow
And relieve your minds and your hearts;
For this morning I saw tears streaming from your eyes.'
3630 The Franks reply: 'Lord, this we must do.'
Each man strikes the mightiest blows he can muster;
Of those who are there few escaped.

270

The heat is great and the dust rises;
The pagans flee and the Franks press them hard.
The chase lasts as far as Saragossa.   3635
Bramimonde has climbed to the top of her tower,
Together with her clerks and her canons,
Whose false faith God never loved.
They have no orders and their heads are not tonsured.
When she saw the Arabs destroyed,   3640
She exclaims in a loud voice: 'Help us, Muhammad!
O, noble king, now our men are vanquished;
The emir is slain with such great shame.'
When Marsile hears her, he turns towards the wall;
He weeps and bows his head low.   3645
He died of grief, oppressed by misfortune;
He gives up his soul to the living devils.   AOI.

271

The pagans are dead, some have turned and fled,
And Charles has won his battle.
He has broken down the gate of Saragossa;   3650
He knows now that it will no longer be defended.
He takes the citadel and his men entered it.
That night they lay there in victory.
Fierce is the king with the hoary-white beard
And Bramimonde surrendered the towers to him.   3655
Ten of them are large, the other fifty small.
He whom the Lord God helps achieves much.

272

The day passes and night has fallen;
The moon is bright and the stars shine forth.
The emperor has taken Saragossa;   3660
He has the city searched by a thousand Franks,
The synagogues and the mosques as well.
With iron hammers and hatchets which they held

They shatter the statues and all the idols.
3665 Neither sorcery nor falseness will be left there.
The king believes in God; he wants to hold a service
And his bishops bless the water.
They take the pagans up to the baptistery;
If there is anyone who withstands Charles,
3670 He has him hanged or burned or put to death.
More than a hundred thousand are baptized
True Christians, with the exception of the queen.
She will be taken as a captive to fair France;
The king wishes her to become a convert through love.

273

3675 The night passes and the bright dawn appears;
Charles garrisoned the towers of Saragossa.
He left a thousand warriors there;
They guard the city for the emperor.
The king mounts his horse along with all his men
3680 And Bramimonde too, whom he takes as his prisoner.
But his intentions for her are entirely good.
They returned with joy and gladness;
They pass Narbonne with a show of strength,
He came to Bordeaux, the city of . . .
3685 Upon the altar of Saint Seurin the baron
He places the oliphant, full of gold and mangons;
Pilgrims who visit the place still see it.
He crosses the Gironde in the great ships found there,
And brought his nephew back as far as Blaye,
3690 And Oliver too, his noble companion,
And the archbishop, who was wise and valiant.
In white coffins he has the lords placed.
The barons lie there in the church of Saint Romain;
The Franks commend them to God and his names.*
3695 Charles rides through the valleys and mountains.
He refuses to halt until they reach Aix;
He rode until he dismounts at the block.
When he is in his lofty palace,

He sends his messengers to summon his judges:
Bavarians and Saxons, men from Lorraine and Frisians. 3700
He summons Germans and he summons Burgundians
And Poitevins and Normans and Bretons,
Together with the wisest men from France.
At this time the trial of Ganelon begins.

274

The emperor has returned from Spain 3705
And he comes to Aix, the principal seat of France.
He goes up to the palace and came into the hall.
See now, Aude came to him, a beautiful girl.
She said to the king: 'Where is Roland the captain,
Who swore to take me as his bride?' 3710
Charles is overcome with grief and distress;
He weeps and tugs at his white beard:
'Sister, dear friend, you ask me about a dead man.
I shall give you a very fine replacement:
That is Louis, I do not know of better. 3715
He is my son and he will rule my kingdom.'
Aude replies: 'These are terrible words.
May it not please God or his saints or his angels,
That I live on after Roland's death!'
Drained of colour she falls at Charlemagne's feet. 3720
She died at once, may God have mercy on her soul!
The Frankish barons weep for her and mourn her.

275

Aude the beautiful has gone to her end;
The king thinks that she has fainted.
The emperor feels pity for her and weeps; 3725
He takes her by the hands and raised her up.
Her head is drooped over her shoulder.
When Charles sees that he has found her dead,
He called at once for four countesses.
She is taken away to a convent of nuns; 3730

That night they watch over her until dawn.
They buried her nobly beside an altar;
The king gave the convent a large gift of land.　　　　AOI.

276

The emperor has returned to Aix;
3735　Ganelon the traitor, in iron chains,
Is in the citadel before the palace.
The servants have tied him to a post;
They bind his hands with thongs of deer-hide
And beat him thoroughly with sticks and staves.
3740　He has not deserved a different fate;
In great anguish he awaits his trial there.

277

It is written in the ancient chronicle
That Charles summons vassals from many lands.
They are assembled in the chapel in Aix.
3745　The day is solemn, the festival is great;
Many say it was Saint Sylvester's day.
Then the trial and the case begin
Of Ganelon who committed treason.
The emperor had him dragged before him.　　　　AOI.

278

3750　'Lord barons,' said King Charlemagne,
'Give me a true judgement with regard to Ganelon.
He came with me in my army as far as Spain
And robbed me of twenty thousand of my Franks
And my nephew, whom you will never see again,
3755　Oliver too, the brave and the courtly.
He betrayed the twelve peers for money.'
Ganelon said: 'A curse on me, if I conceal this!
Roland wronged me in respect of gold and wealth;
For which reason I sought his death and his woe.

But I admit to no treason in this act.' 3760
The Franks reply: 'Now we shall hold a council.'

279

Ganelon stood there before the king;
His body is robust, his face of noble hue;
If he were loyal, he would seem the perfect baron.
He sees the men of France and all the judges 3765
And thirty of his kinsmen who are with him.
Then he shouted out loudly in clear tones:
'For the love of God, listen to me, barons.
Lords, I was in the army with the emperor;
I served him in faith and in love. 3770
Roland his nephew conceived a hatred for me
And nominated me for death and woe.
I was a messenger to King Marsile;
Through my wisdom I managed to escape.
I challenged Roland the warrior 3775
And Oliver and all his companions;
Charles heard it and his noble barons.
I avenged myself, but there is no treason in it.'
The Franks reply: 'We shall begin our council.'

280

When Ganelon sees that his great trial is under way, 3780
He had thirty of his kinsmen with him;
There is one to whom the others pay attention:
He is Pinabel from Castel de Sorence.
He is a skilled talker and a good spokesman
And also a good vassal for defending his arms.* AOI. 3785

281

Ganelon said: 'In you . . . friend . . .
Now save me from death and from this accusation.'
Pinabel said: 'You will soon be free.

There is no Frank who dares sentence you to hang,
3790 To whom, if the emperor brings us together,
I shall not give the lie with my steel sword.'
In thanks Count Ganelon kneels at his feet.

282

Bavarians and Saxons have gone to the council
And Poitevins and Normans and Franks.
3795 There are many Germans and Teutons there.
Those from the Auvergne are the most skilled in law;
Because of Pinabel they are inclined to peace.*
They said to each other: 'It is best to let matters drop.
Let us abandon the trial and beseech the king
3800 To absolve Ganelon this time;
Let him then serve him in love and faith.
Roland is dead, never will you see him again.
He will not be recovered for gold or any sum of money;
Anyone who fought over this would be a fool.'
3805 There is no one who does not grant this and agree,
Except for Thierry, the brother of Lord Geoffrey.   AOI.

283

Charlemagne's barons return to him;
They say to the king: 'Lord, we beseech you
To absolve Count Ganelon,
3810 Then let him serve you in faith and love.
Let him live, for he is a very noble man.
Never, even if he dies, will this baron be seen again*
And no amount of money will ever get him back for us.'
The king said: 'You are traitors to me.'   AOI.

284

3815 When Charles sees that everyone has failed him,
He bows his head and keeps his face down low;
The sorrow he feels makes him bewail his fate.

But see, before him stands a knight, Thierry,
The brother of Geoffrey, a duke of Anjou.
His body was spare and slim and slender,   3820
His hair black and his face somewhat tanned.
He is not big, but nor is he too small.
In courtly fashion he spoke to the emperor:
'Fair lord king, do not distress yourself so.
You know that I have served you very well;   3825
By virtue of my ancestors I must make this case:
Whatever Roland may have done to Ganelon,
The act of serving you should have protected him.
Ganelon is a traitor in that he betrayed him;
He committed perjury against you and wronged you.   3830
For this I judge that he be hanged and put to death
And his body should be placed . . .
As befits a man who has committed treason.
If he now has a kinsman who would give me the lie,
With this sword I have girded on   3835
I am willing to uphold my verdict at once.'
The Franks reply: 'You have spoken well.'

285

Pinabel then came before the king.
He is tall and strong, brave and swift;
The man he strikes has come to the end of his days.   3840
He said to the king: 'Lord, this trial is yours;
Order that this confusion should cease.
I see Thierry here who has given judgement;
I declare it false and shall do battle with him.'
He places in the king's hand his right deerskin gauntlet;   3845
The emperor said: 'I required good surety.'
So thirty kinsmen make a pledge of loyalty;
The king said: 'And I shall set him at liberty.'
He has them guarded until the trial takes place.   AOI.

286

3850 When Thierry sees that there will now be a battle,
He presented his right gauntlet to Charles.
The emperor secures him with hostages;
Then he has four benches brought on to the spot.
Those who are to fight take their seats there;
3855 They are summoned to battle by the agreement of the rest.
Ogier of Denmark explained the procedures;
And then they ask for their horses and their arms.

287

Now that the battle is arranged,   AOI.
They make confession and are absolved and blessed.
3860 They hear mass and receive communion
And place generous offerings in the churches.
Then they both came back before Charles.
They have their spurs fitted to their feet
And don shining hauberks, strong and light;
3865 Their bright helmets are fastened upon their heads.
They gird on their swords with pommels of pure gold;
Around their necks they hang their quartered shields
And in their right hands they carry their sharp spears.
Then they mounted their swift war-horses,
3870 Whereupon a hundred thousand knights began to weep.
Because of Roland they feel pity for Thierry.
God well knows how it will all end.

288

Beneath Aix the meadow is very broad;
The combat between the two barons has begun.
3875 They are valiant men of great courage
And their horses are swift and lively.
They spur them on well, letting go the reins;
With all their might they go to strike each other.
Their entire shields are shattered and smashed;
3880 They tear their hauberks and burst their saddle girths.

Their bows are turned round and their saddles fall;
A hundred thousand men weep as they watch them.

289

Both the knights are together on the ground,   AOI.
Swiftly they jump back on to their feet.
Pinabel is strong and swift and agile;   3885
They attack each other without their horses.
With swords whose pommels are of pure gold
They strike repeatedly on their steel helmets.
Mighty are the blows which tear apart the helmets;
Great is the lament of the Frankish knights.   3890
'O God,' said Charles, 'make justice shine forth!'

290

Pinabel said: 'Thierry, surrender;
I shall become your vassal in love and faith
And shall give you as much as you desire of my wealth.
But let Ganelon be reconciled with the king.'   3895
Thierry replies: 'I shall not hear of it.
A curse on me, if I ever agree to this.
Let God show this day which of us is right.'   AOI.

291

Thierry said: 'Pinabel, you are very brave;
You are tall and strong and your body is well formed.   3900
Your peers recognize your courage.
Let this combat cease right now;
I shall reconcile you with Charlemagne.
Justice will be done to Ganelon;
No day will dawn without it being spoken of.'   3905
Pinabel said: 'May the Lord God forbid!
I want to support all my kinsmen
And shall not surrender for any man alive.
I should sooner die than be reproached for this.'

3910 With their swords they renew their blows
On their helmets, studded with pure gold and gems;
Bright sparks fly up towards heaven.
It is not possible to separate them now;
Only when one of them is dead will the battle end.   AOI.

292

3915 Pinabel of Sorence is very brave
And he strikes Thierry on his helmet from Provence;
The sparks fly on to the grass, setting it alight.
The point of his sword of steel bears down
On his forehead . . .
3920 He brings it right down on to his face;
His right cheek is covered in blood.
His hauberk is burst open right down to his waist;
God protects him from being cast down dead.   AOI.

293

Thierry sees that he is wounded in the face;
3925 The clear blood falls on to the grassy meadow.
He strikes Pinabel on his helmet of burnished steel;
He broke and split it right down to the nasal.
His brains spilled forth from his head;
Thierry raised his sword and flung him dead.
3930 With this blow the combat is won.
The Franks shout out: 'God has performed a miracle.
It is right for Ganelon to be hanged
And his kinsmen who upheld his suit.'   AOI.

294

When Thierry has won his combat,
3935 The Emperor Charles came up to him,
Together with forty of his barons.
Duke Naimes, Ogier of Denmark,
Geoffrey of Anjou and William of Blaye.
The king took Thierry in his arms;

He wipes his face with his great marten skins; 3940
He lays these aside, then they put others on him.
They disarm the knight very gently
And sit him astride a mule from Arabia.
He returns in joy and jubilation.
They arrive at Aix and dismount in the square. 3945
At that time the execution of the others commences.

295

Charles addresses his counts and his dukes:
'What is your advice concerning those whom I detained?
They came to support Ganelon in his trial;
For Pinabel they agreed to become hostages.' 3950
The Franks reply: 'Not a single one shall live.'
The king commands his provost, Basbrun:
'Go and hang them all from the gallows-tree.
By this beard whose hair is hoary white,
If one escapes, you are dead and ruined.' 3955
He replies: 'What else could I do?'
With a hundred serving-men he leads them away by force;
There are thirty of them who were hanged.
A traitor kills himself and his fellows. AOI.

296

Then the Bavarians and the Germans came back, 3960
Together with the Poitevins, Bretons and Normans.
Above all others the Franks agreed
That Ganelon should die in terrible agony.
They have four war-horses brought forward;
Then they bind him by his hands and feet. 3965
The horses are mettlesome and swift;
Four servants goad them on
Towards a stream which flows through a field.
Ganelon was given over to total perdition.
All his ligaments are stretched taut 3970
And he is torn limb from limb;

His clear blood spills out on to the green grass.
Ganelon died a traitor's death.
A man who betrays another has no right to boast of it.

297

3975 When the emperor has completed his vengeance,
He addressed the bishops of France
And those of Bavaria and Germany.
'In my house there is a noble captive;
She has heard so many sermons and parables
3980 That, wishing to believe in God, she seeks Christianity.
Baptize her, so that God may have her soul.'
They reply to her: 'May it be done through godmothers,
Very loyal and noble ladies.'*
In the baths at Aix there is a vast gathering;
3985 There they baptize the Queen of Spain.
They found for her the name of Juliana;
She is a Christian, convinced of the truth.

298

When the emperor has completed his justice
And appeased his great anger,
3990 He has Bramimonde christened.
The day passes, the night has fallen;
The king lay in his vaulted chamber.
Saint Gabriel came to him in God's name:
'Charles, summon your imperial armies.
3995 You will invade the land of Bire,
And help King Vivien in Imphe,
The city which the pagans have besieged.
The Christians call upon you and cry out for you.'
The emperor had no wish to go.
4000 'God,' said the king, 'how wearisome my life is!'
He weeps and tugs at his white beard.
Here ends the story which Turoldus relates.

Notes

45. The terms *onur* and *deintét* in this line are difficult to translate. In addition to the concept of honour, very much bound up at this time with land, the term *onur* may refer to the land of Spain itself and *deintét* to the rights which possession of this land confers.

300–301. These lines are variously interpreted. Is Ganelon announcing that he will commit an act of recklessness (*legerie*) before he goes to King Marsile, while he is with him, or after he returns? Just what will this act be and where will he give vent to his rage? The meaning of *einz . . . que* 'before, rather than' is not clear.

373. Charlemagne did not, of course, conquer England. Has Charles here been assimilated to William the Conqueror? The *chevage* or toll to which the text refers is presumably the payment to Rome of one penny per house for Saint Peter, an annual tribute much discussed at the end of the eleventh century. See Jenkins, pp. 37–8.

400. This line ('*L'emperere meïsmes ad tut a sun talent*') has often been seen as indicating that Charles has everything he wishes from Roland. It has also been suggested that the line tells us that Roland has the emperor entirely under his thumb.

1203–4. It is not clear whether the verb *empeindre* used in v. 1203 and elsewhere indicates that Roland gives his opponent a good push or that he has actually transfixed his opponent by ramming his lance right into his body. The expression *pleine sa hanste*, which occurs eight times in the poem, has been interpreted in many ways: 'with lance at the level', 'a lance-length away from his horse', 'without breaking his lance', 'with outstretched lance', etc. Jenkins interprets as 'a free blow, a blow with the whole length of the spear-handle' (note to v. 1204). It may be that once the opponent had been sent toppling and was powerless to defend himself, a free blow of the lance would be the ultimate humiliation. When he hits the ground, he is then subjected to the further humiliation of insults.

1297. According to the Digby MS it is Gualter who strikes Estorgans. But it is Oton who is the companion of Berenger (see v. 795 and v. 1304).

1389. The MS reading for v. 1388 ('*Espue's icil fut filz burdel*') is not satisfactory and it appears that two lines have been telescoped into one.

1444. Some editors prefer to emend the *ad*, 'has', for the MS to *est*, 'is', and to interpret as 'That our emperor is brave'.

1449. Between v. 1448 and v. 1449 Whitehead indicates two blank lines.

1466–7. At v. 1467 some editors begin to re-order the *laisses* as they are found in the MS.

1652–3. The *laisse* beginning in v. 1653 indicates some of the variations in *laisse* division amongst editors. For Whitehead the new *laisse* is 125a, whereas for Bédier it is 126 (but Bédier reverses the order and makes Whitehead's *laisse* 126 his own 125). Jenkins keeps Whitehead's order but does not create a new *laisse* at v. 1653. Jenkins begins *laisse* 125 at v. 1661.

1863. Commentators argue about the meaning of *pur mei* ('for me' or 'because of me'?).

1926. I have accepted the emendation *cors*, 'bodies', for *mors*, 'deaths'.

2075. This line has fifteen syllables in the MS. Whitehead introduces a new line 2075a. Some editors suppress the final weapon mentioned, the *gieser* (a form of spear).

2832. Readings for this line vary. See Whitehead, p. 126.

2900. Should one read this line with Whitehead as '*Cum en Espaigne venis [a] mal seignur!*' ('How you came to a bad lord in Spain!') or with Brault as '*Cum en Espaigne venis mal, seignur!*' ('How you came badly / ill to Spain, lord!')?

3146. The scribe seems to have inadvertently omitted a reference to the name Preciuse.

3241. The Petchenegs are called Pinceneis in the text and any identification of this and other tribes mentioned here as Baligant's supporters can only be tentative. See the Index of Proper Names and the notes to the relevant lines in Jenkins.

3395. A word is missing after 'until'. Whitehead and Jenkins supply *mort*, 'death'. Bédier prefers *nuit*, 'nightfall'.

3555. Editors vary between saying that the Arabs *s'en turnent*, 'turn away, flee' (Bédier), *s'en turnent plus .C.*, 'more than a hundred flee' (Brault), *s'en contienent plus queit*, 'behave more quietly' (Jenkins) or *s'en tienent plus quei* (Whitehead).

3694. At special moments, particularly in times of danger, it was customary to recite prayers which included an enumeration of the many names of God in Latin, Hebrew or Greek. These names were considered to possess special powers.

3785. To defend one's armour was not to be defeated, not to give an opponent a chance to remove a victim's valuable equipment.

3796–7. Translations of these lines vary. I have taken *curteis* to mean 'skilled in law', not 'courteous' or 'inclined to clemency', etc.

3812. Readings vary for this line. See Jenkins, pp. 265–6, and Brault, II, pp. 280–81.

3983. A difficult line. The meanings for the terms *cruiz* and *linees* are uncertain.

Glossary of Unusual Terms

ALMAÇOR. A Saracen title of honour, chieftain.

AMETHYST. A clear purple or bluish-violet gemstone.

BARON. A feudal landowner and counsellor. Not a specific rank. Its use often suggests bravery and the possession of the qualities required by feudal society.

BEZANT. A Byzantine gold coin, identical with the Roman solidus. First issued under Constantine.

BLOCK. The block of stone used by riders for mounting and dismounting.

BOSS. A circular protuberance, especially ornamented, on a shield.

BOWS. Saddle-bows, the pommel of a saddle.

BUCKLER. A small round shield.

BYRNIE. A leather or padded coat or cuirass often covered with metal plates or rings (see Hauberk).

CALIPH. The title of the successors of Muhammad as rulers of the Islamic world.

CARBUNCLE. A red gemstone (ruby) presented as being endowed with the capacity to emit a light in the dark.

CHARNEL-HOUSE. A building for the deposit of corpses or bones.

COIF. A leather or steel cap worn under the helmet.

DROMOND. A large, swift sailing vessel.

EMIR. Ruler or chieftain of the Islamic world.

ESTERMINAL. A sort of precious stone (an attempt to render the Old French *esterminals*).

FIEF. A vassal's reward from his lord for service. Normally a piece of land, but can refer to a variety of ways of providing financial assistance for a knight. In v. 866 the term *feu*, 'fief', alludes to the privilege of striking the first blow against Roland.

HAUBERK. A coat of mail. Can consist of double or triple links of mail (see v. 995). Seems not to be clearly distinguished in this poem from the byrnie.

HONOUR. Can refer specifically to lands and be more or less the equivalent of fief.

JACINTH. A gemstone, probably the sapphire. Also called the hyacinth.

LIGHTER. A flat-bottomed barge.

MANGON. A gold coin worth two bezants.

MARCH. Literally border land, frontier province. Seems to be used in a wider sense to mean lands or domain. See Marquis.

MARQUIS. The holder of a march or border territory. May refer more generally to a vassal of high rank.

OLIPHANT. Roland's ivory horn. The term derives from *elephantum*.

ORIFLAMME. A scarlet banner, originally of the abbey of Saint Denis, adopted since Philip I as the battle standard of France. In this poem (v. 3093–4) the oriflamme receives the name Romaine and is the golden banner of the city of Rome.

PALFREY. A light saddle-horse (often used by women) ridden to spare the war-horses.

PENNON. A small flag with tails attached to the end of the lance.

PIMENT. A form of wine. The fermented juice of the grape was converted into piment (*pigmenta*) by compounding it with honey, spices and other aromatics.

POMMEL. The knob on the hilt of a sword or the raised part at the front of a saddle.

SAFFRON. An orange to orange-yellow colour perhaps created by weaving brass into the links of the hauberk or byrnie (vv. 1032, 1372, 2499, 3141, 3307, *desaffret*, 3426). Whitehead translates *saf(f)ret* as 'damascened', which would presumably imply inlaying with gold. Jenkins interprets as 'blue-bordered'.

SARDONYX. A gemstone alternately banded in red and white or yellow. A variety of onyx or chalcedony.

SUMPTER. A pack-horse.

THYMIAMA. A form of incense.

VANTAIL. An adjustable part of a helmet as covering for the lower part of the face. Allows the admission of fresh air.

WIGAR. A type of javelin (an attempt to render Old French *wigre*).

Bibliography

For more complete lists of items consult Joseph J. Duggan, *A Guide to Studies on the Chanson de Roland* (London, Grant & Cutler, 1976), Brault, vol. I, pp. 479–510 (see below) and the now annual issues of the *Bulletin Bibliographique de la Société Rencesvals* (Paris, Nizet, 1958–   ).

EDITIONS

Since its publication in 1837 by Francisque Michel the poem has been frequently edited. Readers may wish to consult in particular:

Bédier, Joseph, *La Chanson de Roland* (Paris, Piazza, 1921, definitive edition, 1937). Frequently reprinted. Contains a translation into French.

Brault, Gerard J., *The Song of Roland: an Analytical Edition*, vol. II, Oxford text and English translation (University Park, Pennsylvania, and London, Pennsylvania State University Press, 1978).

Jenkins, T. Atkinson, *La Chanson de Roland: Oxford Version* (Boston, London, etc., 1924, revised 1929, reprinted, with a bibliographical supplement by G. J. Brault, American Life Foundation, 1977). Excellent notes and glossary.

Jonin, Pierre, *La Chanson de Roland* (Paris, Gallimard, Collection Folio, 1979). Contains a translation into French.

Mortier, Raoul, *Les Textes de la Chanson de Roland*, 10 vols (Paris, La Geste Francor, 1940–44). Provides a text of all the French versions of the poem.

Segre, Cesare, *La Chanson de Roland* (Milan and Naples, Ricciardi, 1971). An excellent text with copious supporting documentation.

Short, Ian, *La Chanson de Roland* (Paris, Le Livre de Poche, 1990, 2nd ed., 1994). Contains a text with facing translation into French.

Whitehead, Frederick, *La Chanson de Roland* (Oxford, Blackwell, 1942; 2nd ed., 1946, reissued with an introduction by T. D. Hemming,

Bristol, Bristol Classical Press, 1993). This edition has been used as the basis for the present translation.

BOOKS

Bédier, Joseph, *La Chanson de Roland commentée* (Paris, Piazza, 1927, reprinted 1968). Often known as *Commentaires*. Contains an excellent glossary by Lucien Foulet, pp. 323–501.

Boissonnade, Prosper, *Du Nouveau sur la Chanson de Roland: La genèse historique, le cadre géographique, le milieu, les personnages, la date et l'auteur du poème* (Paris, Champion, 1923).

Brault, Gerard J., *The Song of Roland: an Analytical Edition*, vol. I, Introduction and Commentary (University Park, Pennsylvania and London, Pennsylvania State University Press, 1978). An immensely detailed commentary (574 pp.).

Burger, André, *Turold, poète de la fidélité: essai d'explication de la Chanson de Roland* (Geneva, Droz, 1977).

Cook, Robert F., *The Sense of the Song of Roland* (Ithaca, New York, and London, Cornell University Press, 1987).

Duggan, Joseph J., *A Concordance of the Chanson de Roland* (Columbus, Ohio, Ohio State University Press, 1969).

Duggan, Joseph J., *The Song of Roland: Formulaic Style and Poetic Craft* (Berkeley, Los Angeles and London, University of California Press, 1973).

Haidu, Peter, *The Subject of Violence: The Song of Roland and the Birth of the State* (Bloomington, Indiana, 1993).

Jones, George F., *The Ethos of the Song of Roland* (Baltimore, Johns Hopkins Press, 1963).

Le Gentil, Pierre, *La Chanson de Roland* (Paris, Hatier-Boivin, 1955; 2nd ed. 1967). Translated by Frances F. Beer, *The Chanson de Roland* (Cambridge, Mass., Harvard University Press, 1969).

Menéndez Pidal, Ramón, *La Chanson de Roland et la tradition épique des Francs*, translated by I.-M. Cluzel (Paris, Picard, 2nd ed., 1960).

Pensom, Roger, *Literary Technique in the Chanson de Roland* (Geneva, Droz, 1982).

Rychner, Jean, *La Chanson de geste: essai sur l'art épique des jongleurs* (Geneva, Droz, and Lille, Giard, 1955).

Van Emden, Wolfgang, *La Chanson de Roland* (London, Grant and Cutler, 1995).

Vance, Eugene, *Reading the Song of Roland* (Englewood Cliffs, New Jersey, Prentice-Hall, 1970).

La Chanson de Roland

The Betrayal

1

Carles li reis, nostre emperere magnes,
Set anz tuz pleins ad estét en Espaigne.
Tresqu'en la mer cunquist la tere altaigne;
N'i ad castel ki devant lui remaigne,
5   Mur ne citét n'i est remés a fraindre,
Fors Sarraguce, ki est en une muntaigne.
Li reis Marsilie la tient, ki Deu nen aimet;
Mahumet sert e Apollin recleimet.
Nes poet guarder que mals ne l'i ateignet.   AOI.

2

10   Li reis Marsilie esteit en Sarraguce;
Alez en est en un verger suz l'umbre.
Sur un perrun de marbre bloi se culchet,
Envirun lui plus de vint milie humes.
Il en apelet e ses dux e ses cuntes:
15   'Oëz, seignurs, quel pecchét nus encumbret.
Li empereres Carles de France dulce
En cest païs nos est venuz cunfundre.
Jo nen ai ost qui bataille li dunne,
Ne n'ai tel gent ki la sue derumpet:
20   Cunseilez mei cume mi savie hume,
Si me guarisez e de mort e de hunte.'

164

N'i ad paien ki un sul mot respundet,
Fors Blancandrins de Castel de Valfunde.

3

Blancandrins fut des plus saives paiens;
De vasselage fut asez chevaler,   25
Prozdom i out pur sun seignur aider.
E dist al rei: 'Ore ne vus esmaiez;
Mandez Carlun, a l'orguillus e al fier,
Fedeilz servises e mult granz amistez:
Vos li durrez urs e leons e chens,   30
Set cenz camelz e mil hosturs müers,
D'or e d'argent ·iiii· c· muls cargez,
Cinquante carre qu'en ferat carïer.
Ben en purrat lüer ses soldeiers.
En ceste tere ad asez osteiét;   35
En France ad Ais s'en deit ben repairer.
Vos le sivrez a la feste seint Michel,
Si recevrez la lei de chrestïens;
Serez ses hom par honur e par ben.
S'en volt ostages, e vos l'en enveiez,   40
U dis u vint, pur lui afiancer.
Enveiuns i les filz de noz muillers;
Par nun d'ocire i enveierai le men.
Asez est melz qu'il i perdent les chefs
Que nus perduns l'onur ne la deintét,   45
Ne nus seiuns cunduiz a mendeier.'   AOI.

4

Dist Blancandrins: 'Par ceste meie destre
E par la barbe ki al piz me ventelet,
L'ost des Franceis verrez sempres desfere;
Francs s'en irunt en France, la lur tere.   50
Quant cascuns ert a sun meillor repaire,
Carles serat ad Ais, a sa capele;
A seint Michel tendrat mult halte feste.

Vendrat li jurz, si passerat li termes,
55 N'orrat de nos paroles ne nuveles.
Li reis est fiers e sis curages pesmes;
De noz ostages ferat trencher les testes.
Asez est mielz qu'il i perdent les testes
Que nus perduns clere Espaigne la bele,
60 Ne nus aiuns les mals ne les suffraites.'
Dient paien: 'Issi poet il ben estre.'

5

Li reis Marsilie out sun cunseill finét,
Sin apelat Clarin de Balaguét,
Estamarin e Eudropin sun per
65 E Priamun e Guarlan le barbét
E Machiner e sun uncle Maheu
E Joüner e Malbien d'ultre mer
E Blancandrins por la raisun cunter.
Des plus feluns dis en ad apelez:
70 'Seignurs baruns, a Carlemagnes irez;
Il est al siege a Cordres la citét.
Branches d'olives en voz mains porterez:
Ço senefiet pais e humilitét.
Par voz saveirs sem püez acorder,
75 Jo vos durrai or e argent asez,
Teres e fiez tant cum vos en vuldrez.'
Dient paien: 'De ço avun nus asez.'   AOI.

6

Li reis Marsilie out finét sun cunseill.
Dist a ses humes: 'Seignurs, vos en ireiz;
80 Branches d'olive en voz mains portereiz,
Si me direz a Carlemagne le rei,
Pur le soen Deu, qu'il ait mercit de mei.
Ja einz ne verrat passer cest premer meis
Que jel sivrai od mil de mes fedeilz,
85 Si recevrai la chrestïene lei.

Serai ses hom par amur e par feid;
S'il voelt ostages, il en avrat par veir.'
Dist Blancandrins: 'Mult bon plait en avreiz.'   AOI.

7

Dis blanches mules fist amener Marsilies
Que li tramist li reis de Suatilie;   90
Li frein sunt d'or, les seles d'argent mises.
Cil sunt muntez ki le message firent;
Enz en lur mains portent branches d'olive.
Vindrent a Charles, ki France ad en baillie;
Nes poet guarder que alques ne l'engignent.   AOI.   95

8

Li empereres se fait e balz e liez;
Cordres ad prise e les murs peceiez,
Od ses cadables les turs en abatiéd.
Mult grant eschech en unt si chevaler
D'or e d'argent e de guarnemenz chers.   100
En la citét nen ad remés paien
Ne seit ocis u devient chrestïen.
Li empereres est en un grant verger,
Ensembl'od lui Rollant e Oliver,
Sansun li dux e Anseïs li fiers,   105
Gefreid d'Anjou, le rei gunfanuner,
E si i furent e Gerin e Gerers;
La u cist furent des altres i out bien.
De dulce France i ad quinze milliers;
Sur palies blancs siedent cil cevaler.   110
As tables juent pur els esbaneier
E as eschecs li plus saive e li veill,
E escremissent cil bacheler leger.
Desuz un pin, delez un eglenter,
Un faldestoed i unt fait tut d'or mer;   115
La siet li reis ki dulce France tient.
Blanche ad la barbe e tut flurit le chef,

Gent ad le cors e le cuntenant fier;
S'est kil demandet, ne l'estoet enseigner.
120 E li message descendirent a pied,
Sil saluerent par amur e par bien.

9

Blancandrins ad tut premereins parléd
E dist al rei: 'Salvét seiez de Deu,
Le glorïus que devuns aürer.
125 Iço vus mandet reis Marsilies li bers:
Enquis ad mult la lei de salvetét;
De sun aveír vos voelt asez duner,
Urs e leüns e veltres enchaignez,
Set cenz cameilz e mil hosturs müez,
130 D'or e d'argent ·iiii· cenz muls trussez,
Cinquante care que carier en ferez.
Tant i avrat de besanz esmerez
Dunt bien purrez voz soldeiers lüer;
En cest païs avez estét asez.
135 En France, ad Ais, devez bien repairer;
La vos sivrat, ço dit, mis avoëz.'
Li empereres tent ses mains vers Deu;
Baisset sun chef, si cumencet a penser.   AOI.

10

Li empereres en tint sun chef enclin.
140 De sa parole ne fut mie hastifs;
Sa custume est qu'il parolet a leisir.
Quant se redrecet, mult par out fier lu vis;
Dist as messages: 'Vus avez mult ben dit.
Li reis Marsilies est mult mis enemis;
145 De cez paroles que vos avez ci dit
En quel mesure en purrai estre fiz?'
'Voelt par hostages,' ço dist li Sarrazins,
'Dunt vos avrez u dis u quinze u vint.
Par nun de ocire i metrai un mien filz,

E si n'avrez, ço quid, de plus gentilz.   150
Quant vus serez el palais seignurill,
A la grant feste seint Michel del Peril,
Mis avoëz la vos sivrat, ço dit.
Enz en voz bainz, que Deus pur vos i fist,
La vuldrat il chrestïens devenir.'   155
Charles respunt: 'Uncore purrat guarir.'   AOI.

                              11
Bels fut li vespres e li soleilz fut cler;
Les dis mulez fait Charles establer.
El grant verger fait li reis tendre un tref;
Les dis messages ad fait enz hosteler;   160
·xii· serjanz les unt ben cunreez.
La noit demurent tresque vint al jur cler;
Li empereres est par matin levét,
Messe e matines ad li reis escultét.
Desuz un pin en est li reis alez,   165
Ses baruns mandet pur sun cunseill finer.
Par cels de France voelt il del tut errer.   AOI.

                              12
Li empereres s'en vait desuz un pin.
Ses baruns mandet pur sun cunseill fenir:
Le duc Oger e l'arcevesque Turpin,   170
Richard li velz e sun nevuld Henri,
E de Gascuigne li proz quens Acelin,
Tedbald de Reins e Milun, sun cusin,
E si i furent e Gerers e Gerin;
Ensembl'od els li quens Rollant i vint   175
E Oliver, li proz e li gentilz.
Des Francs de France en i ad plus de mil;
Guenes i vint, ki la traïsun fist.
Des ore cumencet le cunseill que mal prist.   AOI.

                             169

13

180 'Seignurs barons,' dist li emperere Carles,
'Li reis Marsilie m'ad tramis ses messages.
De sun aveir me voelt duner grant masse:
Urs e leüns e veltres caeignables,
Set cenz cameilz e mil hosturs muables,
185 Quatre cenz muls cargez de l'or d'Arabe;
Avoec iço plus de cinquante care.
Mais il me mandet que en France m'en alge;
Il me sivrat ad Ais, a mun estage,
Si recevrat la nostre lei plus salve.
190 Chrestïens ert, de mei tendrat ses marches;
Mais jo ne sai quels en est sis curages.'
Dient Franceis: 'Il nus i cuvent guarde.'   AOI.

14

Li empereres out sa raisun fenie;
Li quens Rollant, ki ne l'otriet mie,
195 En piez se drecet, si li vint cuntredire.
Il dist al rei: 'Ja mar crerez Marsilie.
Set anz ad pleins que en Espaigne venimes;
Jo vos cunquis e Noples e Commibles,
Pris ai Valterne e la tere de Pine
200 E Balasguéd e Tüele e Sezilie.
Li reis Marsilie i fist mult que traïtre;
De ses paiens enveiat quinze,
Chascuns portout une branche d'olive.
Nuncerent vos cez paroles meïsme;
205 A voz Franceis un cunseill en presistes.
Loërent vos alques de legerie;
Dous de voz cuntes al paien tramesistes,
L'un fut Basan e li altres Basilies.
Les chefs en prist es puis desuz Haltilie.
210 Faites la guerre cum vos l'avez enprise;
En Sarraguce menez vostre ost banie.
Metez le sege a tute vostre vie,
Si vengez cels que li fels fist ocire.'   AOI.

15

Li emperere en tint sun chef enbrunc,
Si duist sa barbe, afaitad sun gernun;   215
Ne ben ne mal ne respunt sun nevuld.
Franceis se taisent ne mais que Guenelun;
En piez se drecet, si vint devant Carlun.
Mult fierement cumencet sa raisun
E dist al rei: 'Ja mar crerez bricun,   220
Ne mei ne altre, se de vostre prod nun.
Quant ço vos mandet li reis Marsiliun
Qu'il devendrat jointes ses mains tis hom
E tute Espaigne tendrat par vostre dun,
Puis recevrat la lei que nus tenum,   225
Ki ço vos lodet que cest plait degetuns,
Ne li chalt, sire, de quel mort nus murjuns.
Cunseill d'orguill n'est dreiz que a plus munt;
Laissun les fols, as sages nus tenuns.'   AOI.

16

Aprés iço i est Neimes venud;   230
Meillor vassal n'aveit en la curt nul,
E dist al rei: 'Ben l'avez entendud.
Guenes li quens ço vus ad respondud;
Savier i ad, mais qu'il seit entendud.
Li reis Marsilie est de guere vencud;   235
Vos li avez tuz ses castels toluz,
Od voz caables avez fruisét ses murs,
Ses citez arses e ses humes vencuz;
Quant il vos mandet qu'aiez mercit de lui,
Pecchét fereit ki dunc li fesist plus.   240
U par ostage vos en voelt faire soürs,
Ceste grant guerre ne deit munter a plus.'
Dient Franceis: 'Ben ad parlét li dux.'   AOI.

17

'Seignurs baruns, qui i enveieruns
245 En Sarraguce al rei Marsiliuns?'
Respunt dux Neimes: 'Jo irai, par vostre dun;
Livrez m'en ore le guant e le bastun.'
Respunt li reis: 'Vos estes saives hom;
Par ceste barbe e par cest men gernun,
250 Vos n'irez pas uan de mei si luign.
Alez sedeir, quant nuls ne vos sumunt.'

18

'Seignurs baruns, qui i purruns enveier,
Al Sarrazin ki Sarraguce tient?'
Respunt Rollant: 'Jo i puis aler mult ben.'
255 'Nu ferez certes,' dist li quens Oliver;
'Vostre curages est mult pesmes e fiers.
Jo me crendreie que vos vos meslisez;
Se li reis voelt, jo i puis aler ben.'
Respunt li reis: 'Ambdui vos en taisez;
260 Ne vos ne il n'i porterez les piez.
Par ceste barbe que veez blancheier,
Li duze per mar i serunt jugez.'
Franceis se taisent, as les vus aquisez.

19

Turpins de Reins en est levét del renc
265 E dist al rei: 'Laisez ester voz Francs;
En cest païs avez estét set anz.
Mult unt oüd e peines e ahans;
Dunez m'en, sire, le bastun e le guant
E jo irai al Sarazin espan,
270 Sin vois vedeir alques de sun semblant.'
Li empereres respunt par maltalant:
'Alez sedeir desur cel palie blanc;
N'en parlez mais, se jo nel vos cumant.'   AOI.

20

'Francs chevalers,' dist li emperere Carles,
'Car m'eslisez un barun de ma marche   275
Qu'a Marsiliun me portast mun message.'
Ço dist Rollant: 'Ço ert Guenes, mis parastre.'
Dient Franceis: 'Car il le poet ben faire;
Se lui lessez, n'i trametrez plus saive.'
E li quens Guenes en fut mult anguisables;   280
De sun col getet ses grandes pels de martre
E est remés en sun blialt de palie.
Vairs out les oilz e mult fier lu visage;
Gent out le cors e les costez out larges.
Tant par fut bels tuit si per l'en esguardent.   285
Dist a Rollant: 'Tut fol, pur quei t'esrages?
Ço set hom ben que jo sui tis parastres,
Si as jugét qu'a Marsiliun en alge.
Se Deus ço dunet que jo de la repaire,
Jo t'en muvrai un si grant contraire   290
Ki durerat a trestut tun edage.'
Respunt Rollant: 'Orgoill oi e folage;
Ço set hom ben n'ai cure de manace.
Mais saives hom, il deit faire message.
Si li reis voelt, prez sui por vus le face.'   295

21

Guenes respunt: 'Pur mei n'iras tu mie;   A O I.
Tu n'ies mes hom ne jo ne sui tis sire.
Carles comandet que face sun servise.
En Sarraguce en irai a Marsilie;
Einz i frai un poi de legerie   300
Que jo n'esclair ceste meie grant ire.'
Quant l'ot Rollant, si cumençat a rire.   A O I.

22

Quant ço veit Guenes que ore s'en rit Rollant,
Dunc ad tel doel pur poi d'ire ne fent;
A ben petit que il ne pert le sens.   305

E dit al cunte: 'Jo ne vus aim nïent;
Sur mei avez turnét fals jugement.
Dreiz emperere, veiz me ci en present;
Ademplir voeill vostre comandement.

23

310 'En Sarraguce sai ben que aler m'estoet;   AOI.
Hom ki la vait repairer ne s'en poet.
Ensurquetut si ai jo vostre soer,
Sin ai un filz, ja plus bels nen estoet;
Ço est Baldewin,' ço dit, 'ki ert prozdoem.
315 A lui lais jo mes honurs e mes fieus;
Guardez le ben, ja nel verrai des oilz.'
Carles respunt: 'Trop avez tendre coer;
Puis quel comant, aler vus en estoet.'

24

Ço dist li reis: 'Güenes, venez avant,   AOI.
320 Si recevez le bastun e lu guant;
Oït l'avez, sur vos le jugent Franc.'
'Sire,' dist Guenes, 'ço ad tut fait Rollant;
Ne l'amerai a trestut mun vivant,
Ne Oliver, por ço qu'il est si cumpainz,
325 Li duze per, por qu'il l'aiment tant.
Desfi les ci, sire, vostre veiant.'
Ço dist li reis: 'Trop avez maltalant,
Or irez vos certes, quant jol cumant.'
'Jo i puis aler, mais n'i avrai guarant;   AOI.
330 Nul out Basilies ne sis freres Basant.'

25

Li empereres li tent sun guant, le destre,
Mais li quens Guenes iloec ne volsist estre.
Quant le dut prendre, si li caït a tere.
Dient Franceis: 'Deus, que purrat ço estre?

De cest message nos avendrat grant perte.'   335
'Seignurs,' dist Guenes, 'vos en orrez noveles.'

26

'Sire,' dist Guenes, 'dunez mei le cungiéd;
Quant aler dei, n'i ai plus que targer.'
Ço dist li reis: 'Al Jhesu e al mien.'
De sa main destre l'ad asols e seignét;   340
Puis li livrat le bastun e le bref.

27

Guenes li quens s'en vait a sun ostel;
De guarnemenz se prent a cunreer,
De ses meillors que il pout recuvrer.
Esperuns d'or ad en ses piez fermez,   345
Ceint Murglies s'espee a sun costéd.
En Tachebrun, sun destrer, est muntéd;
L'estreu li tint sun uncle Guinemer.
La veïsez tant chevaler plorer
Ki tuit li dient: 'Tant mare fustes ber!   350
En la cort al rei mult i avez estéd;
Noble vassal vos i solt hom clamer.
Ki tuit li dient: 'Tant mare fustes, ber!
Par Charlemagne n'ert guariz ne tensez.
Li quens Rollant nel se doüst penser,   355
Que estrait estes de mult grant parentéd.'
Enprés li dient: 'Sire, car nos menez.'
Ço respunt Guenes: 'Ne placet Damnedeu;
Mielz est que sul moerge que tant bon chevaler.
En dulce France, seignurs, vos en irez;   360
De meie part ma muiller salüez
E Pinabel, mun ami e mun per,
E Baldewin, mun filz que vos savez,
E lui aidez e pur seignur le tenez.'
Entret en sa veie, si s'est achiminez.   AOI.   365

175

28

Guenes chevalchet suz une olive halte;
Asemblét s'est as Sarrazins messages.
Mais Blancandrins ki envers lu s'atarget.
Par grant saveir parolet li uns a l'altre.
370 Dist Blancandrins: 'Merveilus hom est Charles,
Ki cunquist Puille e trestute Calabre;
Vers Engletere passat il la mer salse,
Ad oes seint Pere en cunquist le chevage;
Que nus requert ça en la nostre marche?'
375 Guenes respunt: 'Itels est sis curages;
Jamais n'ert hume ki encuntre lui vaille.'   AOI.

29

Dist Blancandrins: 'Francs sunt mult gentilz home;
Mult grant mal funt e cil duc e cil cunte
A lur seignur, ki tel cunseill li dunent.
380 Lui e altrui travaillent e cunfundent.'
Guenes respunt: 'Jo ne sai veirs nul hume,
Ne mes Rollant, ki uncore en avrat hunte.
Er matin sedeit li emperere suz l'umbre,
Vint i ses nies, out vestue sa brunie,
385 E out predét dejuste Carcasonie;
En sa main tint une vermeille pume:
"Tenez, bel sire," dist Rollant a sun uncle,
"De trestuz reis vos present les curunes."
Li soens orgoilz le devreit ben cunfundre,
390 Kar chascun jur de mort s'abandunet.
Seit ki l'ociet, tute pais puis avriumes.'   AOI.

30

Dist Blancandrins: 'Mult est pesmes Rollant,
Ki tute gent voelt faire recreant
E tutes teres met en chalengement.
395 Par quele gent quiet il espleiter tant?'
Guenes respunt: 'Par la franceise gent;

Il l'aiment tant, ne li faldrunt nïent.
Or e argent lur met tant en present,
Muls e destrers e palies e guarnemenz.
L'emperere meïsmes ad tut a sun talent; 400
Cunquerrat li les teres d'ici qu'en orïent.' AOI.

31

Tant chevalcherent Guenes e Blancandrins
Que l'un a l'altre la sue feit plevit
Que il querreient que Rollant fust ocis.
Tant chevalcherent e veies e chemins 405
Que en Sarraguce descendent suz un if.
Un faldestoet out suz l'umbre d'un pin;
Envolupét fut d'un palie alexandrin.
La fut li reis ki tute Espaigne tint;
Tut entur lui vint milie Sarrazins, 410
N'i ad celoi ki mot sunt ne mot tint,
Pur les nuveles qu'il vuldreient oïr.
Atant as vos Guenes e Blanchandrins!

32

Blancandrins vint devant Marsiliun;
Par le puign tint le cunte Guenelun 415
E dist al rei: 'Salvez seiez de Mahum
E d'Apollin, qui seintes leis tenuns.
Vostre message fesimes a Charlun;
Ambes ses mains en levat cuntre munt,
Loat sun deu, ne fist altre respuns. 420
Ci vos enveiet un sun noble barun
Ki est de France, si est mult riches hom;
Par lui orrez si avrez pais u nun.'
Respunt Marsilie: 'Or diet, nus l'orrum.' AOI.

33

425 Mais li quens Guenes se fut ben purpensét;
     Par grant saver cumencet a parler,
     Cume celui ki ben faire le set.
     E dist al rei: 'Salvez seiez de Deu,
     Li glorïus qui devum aürer.
430 Iço vus mandet Carlemagnes li ber
     Que recevez seinte chrestïentét;
     Demi Espaigne vos voelt en fiu duner.
     Se cest' acorde ne vulez otrïer,
     Pris e lïez serez par poëstéd.
435 Al siege ad Ais en serez amenét;
     Par jugement serez iloec finét.
     La murrez vus a hunte e a viltét.'
     Li reis Marsilies en fut mult esfreéd;
     Un algier tint, ki d'or fut enpenét;
440 Ferir l'en volt, se n'en fust desturnét.   AOI.

34

     Li reis Marsilies ad la culur müee;
     De sun algeir ad la hanste crollee.
     Quant le vit Guenes, mist la main a l'espee;
     Cuntre dous deie l'ad del furrer getee.
445 Si li ad dit: 'Mult estes bele e clere;
     Tant vus avrai en curt a rei portee,
     Ja nel dirat de France li emperere
     Que suls i moerge en l'estrange cuntree,
     Einz vos avrunt li meillor cumparee.'
450 Dient paien: 'Desfaimes la meslee.'

35

     Tuit li prierent li meillor Sarrazin
     Qu'el faldestoed s'est Marsilies asis.
     Dist l'algalifes: 'Mal nos avez baillit
     Que li Franceis asmastes a ferir;
455 Vos le doüssez esculter e oïr.'

'Sire,' dist Guenes, 'mei l'avent a suffrir;
Jo ne lerreie, por tut l'or que Deus fist,
Ne por tut l'aveir ki seit en cest païs,
Que jo ne li die, se tant ai de leisir,
Que Charles li mandet, li reis poësteïfs,   460
Par mei li mandet, sun mortel enemi.'
Afublez est d'un mantel sabelin
Ki fut cuvert d'un palie alexandrin;
Getet le a tere, sil receit Blancandrin.
Mais de s'espee ne volt mie guerpir;   465
En sun puign destre par l'orie punt la tint.
Dient paien: 'Noble baron ad ci!'   AOI.

36

Envers le rei s'est Guenes aproismét,
Si li ad dit: 'A tort vos curuciez;
Quar ço vos mandet Carles, ki France tient,   470
Que recevez la lei de chrestïens;
Demi Espaigne vus durat il en fiet,
L'altre meitét avrat Rollant sis niés;
Mult orguillos parçuner i avrez.
Si ceste acorde ne volez otrïer,   475
En Sarraguce vus vendrat aseger;
Par poëstét serez pris e lïez.
Menét serez endreit ad Ais le siet;
Vus n'i avrez palefreid ne destrer
Ne mul ne mule que puissez chevalcher,   480
Getét serez sur un malvais sumer;
Par jugement iloec perdrez le chef.
Nostre emperere vus enveiet cest bref.'
El destre poign al paien l'ad livrét.

37
                                                             485
Marsilies fut esculurez de l'ire;
Freint le seel, getét en ad la cire,
Guardet al bref, vit la raisun escrite:

'Carle me mandet, ki France ad en baillie,
Que me remembre de la dolur e de l'ire.
490 Ço est de Basan e de sun frere Basilie,
Dunt pris les chefs as puis de Haltoïe.
Se de mun cors voeil aquiter la vie,
Dunc li envei mun uncle l'algalife;
Altrement ne m'amerat il mie.'
495 Aprés parlat ses filz envers Marsilies
E dist al rei: 'Guenes ad dit folie;
Tant ad errét nen est dreiz que plus vivet.
Livrez le mei, jo en ferai la justise.'
Quant l'oït Guenes, l'espee en ad branlie,
500 Vait s'apuier suz le pin a la tige.

38

Enz el verger s'en est alez li reis,
Ses meillors humes en meinet ensembl'od sei,
E Blancandrins i vint, al canud peil,
E Jurfaret, ki est ses filz e ses heirs
505 E l'algalifes, sun uncle e sis fedeilz.
Dist Blancandrins: 'Apelez le Franceis;
De nostre prod m'ad plevie sa feid.'
Ço dist li reis: 'E vos l'i ameneiz.'
Guenelun prist par la main destre ad deiz;
510 Enz el verger l'en meinet josqu'al rei.
La purparolent la traïsun seinz dreit.   AOI.

39

'Bel sire Guenes,' ço li ad dit Marsilie,
'Jo vos ai fait alques de legerie,
Quant por ferir vus demustrai grant ire.
515 Guaz vos en dreit par cez pels sabelines,
Melz en valt l'or que ne funt cinc cenz livres;
Einz demain noit en iert bele l'amendise.'
Guenes respunt: 'Jo nel desotrei mie;
Deus, se lui plaist, a bien le vos mercie.'   AOI.

40

Ço dist Marsilies: 'Guenes, par veir sacez,   520
En talant ai que mult vos voeill amer;
De Carlemagne vos voeill oïr parler.
Il est mult vielz, si ad sun tens usét,
Men escïent dous cenz anz ad passét;
Par tantes teres ad sun cors demenéd.   525
Tanz colps ad pris sur sun escut bucler,
Tanz riches reis cunduit a mendistéd;
Quant ert il mais recreanz d'osteier?'
Guenes respunt: 'Carles n'est mie tels;
N'est hom kil veit e conuistre le set   530
Que ço ne diet que l'emperere est ber.
Tant nel vos sai ne preiser ne loër
Que plus n'i ad d'onur c dc bontét;
Sa grant valor kil purreit acunter?
De tel barnage l'ad Deus enluminét,   535
Meilz voelt murir que guerpir sun barnét.'

41

Dist li paiens: 'Mult me puis merveiller
De Carlemagne, ki est canuz e vielz,
Men escïentre dous cenz anz ad e mielz.
Par tantes teres ad sun cors traveillét,   540
Tanz cols ad pris de lances e d'espiét,
Tanz riches reis cunduiz a mendistiét;
Quant ert il mais recreanz d'osteier?'
'Ço n'iert,' dist Guenes, 'tant cum vivet sis niés;
N'at tel vassal suz la cape del ciel,   545
Mult par est proz sis cumpainz Oliver.
Les ·xii· pers, que Carles ad tant chers,
Funt les enguardes a ·xx· milie chevalers;
Soürs est Carles, que nuls home ne crent.'   AOI.

42

550   Dist li Sarrazins: 'Merveille en ai grant
De Carlemagne, ki est canuz et blancs;
Mien escïentre plus ad de ·ii·c· anz.
Par tantes teres est alét cunquerant,
Tanz colps ad pris de bons espiez trenchanz,
555   Tanz riches reis morz e vencuz en champ;
Quant iert il mais d'osteier recreant?'
'Ço n'iert,' dist Guenes, 'tant cum vivet Rollant;
N'ad tel vassal d'ici qu'en orïent.
Mult par est proz Oliver sis cumpainz.
560   Li ·xii· per, que Carles aimet tant,
Funt les enguardes a ·xx· milie de Francs;
Soürs est Carles, ne crent hume vivant.'   AOI.

43

'Bel sire Guenes,' dist Marsilies li reis,
'Jo ai tel gent, plus bele ne verreiz;
565   Quatre cenz milie chevalers puis aveir.
Puis m'en cumbatre a Carle e a Franceis?'
Guenes respunt: 'Ne vus a ceste feiz;
De voz paiens mult grant perte i avreiz.
Lessez la folie, tenez vos al saveir.
570   L'empereür tant li dunez aveir
N'i ait Franceis ki tot ne s'en merveilt.
Par ·xx· hostages que li enveiereiz,
En dulce France s'en repairerat li reis.
Sa rereguarde lerrat derere sei;
575   Iert i sis niés, li quens Rollant, ço crei,
E Oliver, li proz e li curteis.
Mort sunt li cunte, se est ki mei en creit.
Carles verrant sun grant orguill cadeir,
N'avrat talent que ja mais vus guerreit.'   AOI.

44

'Bel sire Guenes,' ço dist li reis Marsilies,   580
'Cumfaitement purrai Rollant ocire?'
Guenes respont: 'Ço vos sai jo ben dire.
Li reis serat as meillors porz de Sizer;
Sa rereguarde avrat detrés sei mise,
Iert i sis niés, li quens Rollant li riches,   585
E Oliver en qui il tant se fiet;
·xx· milie Francs unt en lur cumpaignie.
De voz paiens lur enveiez ·c· milie;
Une bataille lur i rendent cil primes.
La gent de France iert blecee e blesmie;   590
Nel di por ço, des voz iert la martirie,
Altre bataille lur livrez de meïsme.
De quel que scit, Rollant n'estoertrat mie.
Dunc avrez faite gente chevalerie;
N'avrez mais guere en tute vostre vie.   AOI. 595

45

Chi purreit faire que Rollant i fust mort,
Dunc perdreit Carles le destre braz del cors,
Si remeindreient les merveilluses oz;
N'asemblereit jamais Carles si grant esforz,
Tere major remeindreit en repos.'   600
Quan l'ot Marsilie, si l'ad baisét el col;
Puis si cumencet a uvrir ses tresors.   AOI.

46

Ço dist Marsilies: 'Qu'en parlereiens mais?
Cunseill n'est proz dunt hume . . .
La traïsun me jurrez de Rollant.'   605
Ço respunt Guenes: 'Issi seit cum vos plaist.'
Sur les reliques de s'espee Murgleis
La traïsun jurat e si s'en est forsfait.   AOI.

47

Un faldestoed i out d'un olifant;
610 Marsilies fait porter un livre avant,
La lei i fut Mahum e Tervagan;
Ço ad jurét li Sarrazins espans:
Se en rereguarde troevet le cors Rollant,
Cumbatrat sei a trestute sa gent,
615 E, se il poet, murrat i veirement.
Guenes respunt: 'Ben seit vostre comant.'   AOI.

48

Atant i vint uns paiens, Valdabruns;
Icil en vait al rei Marsilïun.
Cler en riant l'ad dit a Guenelun:
620 'Tenez m'espee, meillur nen at nuls hom;
Entre les helz ad plus de mil manguns.
Par amistiez, bel sire, la vos duins,
Que nos aidez de Rollant le barun,
Qu'en rereguarde trover le poüsum.'
625 'Ben serat fait,' li quens Guenes respunt;
Puis se baiserent es vis e es mentuns.

49

Aprés i vint un paien, Climorins.
Cler en riant a Guenelun l'ad dit:
'Tenez mun helme, unches meillor ne vi . . .
630 Si nos aidez de Rollant li marchis;
Par quel mesure le poüssum hunir.'
'Ben serat fait,' Guenes respundit;
Puis se baiserent es buches e es vis.   AOI.

50

Atant i vint la reïne Bramimunde:
635 'Jo vos aim mult, sire,' dist ele al cunte,
'Car mult vos priset mi sire e tuit si hume.

A vostre femme enveierai dous nusches:
Bien i ad or, matices e jacunces,
Eles valent mielz que tut l'aveir de Rume;
Vostre emperere si bones ne vit unches.'   640
Il les ad prises, en sa hoese les butet.   AOI.

51

Li reis apelet Malduit, sun tresorer:
'L'aveir Carlun est il apareilliez?'
E cil respunt: 'Oïl, sire, asez bien:
·vii·c· cameilz, d'or e argent cargiez,   645
E ·xx· hostages, des plus gentilz desuz cel.'   AOI.

52

Marsilies tint Guenelun par l'espalle,
Si li ad dit: 'Mult par ies ber e sage;
Par cele lei que vos tenez plus salve,
Guardez de nos ne turnez le curage.   650
De mun aveir vos voeill duner grant masse:
·x· muls cargez del plus fin or d'Arabe,
Ja mais n'iert an altretel ne vos face.
Tenez les clefs de ceste citét large,
Le grant aveir en presentez al rei Carles,   655
Pois me jugez Rollant a rereguarde.
Sel pois trover a port ne a passage,
Liverrai lui une mortel bataille.'
Guenes respunt: 'Mei est vis que trop targe.'
Pois est muntéd, entret en sun veiage.   AOI. 660

53

Li empereres aproismet sun repaire;
Venuz en est a la citét de Galne.
Li quens Rollant, il l'ad e prise e fraite;
Puis icel jur en fut cent anz deserte.
De Guenelun atent li reis nuveles   665

E le treüd d'Espaigne, la grant tere.
Par main en l'albe, si cum li jurz esclairet,
Guenes il quens est venuz as herberges.   AOI.

54

Li empereres est par matin levét;
670 Messe e matines ad li reis escultét.
Sur l'erbe verte estut devant sun tref;
Rollant i fut e Oliver li ber,
Neimes li dux e des altres asez.
Guenes i vint, li fels, li parjurez,
675 Par grant veisdie cumencet a parler
E dist al rei: 'Salvez seiez de Deu;
De Sarraguce ci vos aport les clefs.
Mult grant aveir vos en faz amener
E ·xx· hostages, faites les ben guarder.
680 E si vos mandet reis Marsilies, li ber;
De l'algalifes nel devez pas blasmer;
Kar a mes oilz vi ·iiii·c· milie armez,
Halbers vestuz, alquanz healmes fermez,
Ceintes espees as punz d'or neielez,
685 Ki l'en cunduistrent tresqu'en la mer.
De Marcilie s'en fuient por la chrestïentét
Que il ne voelent ne tenir ne guarder.
Einz qu'il oüssent ·iiii· liues siglét,
Sis aquillit e tempeste e oréd.
690 La sunt neiez, jamais nes en verrez;
Se il fust vif, jo l'oüsse amenét.
Del rei paien, sire, par veir creez,
Ja ne verrez cest premer meis passét
Qu'il vos sivrat en France le regnét,
695 Si recevrat la lei que vos tenez,
Jointes ses mains iert vostre comandét;
De vos tendrat Espaigne le regnét.'
Ço dist li reis: 'Graciét en seit Deus;
Ben l'avez fait, mult grant prod i avrez.'
700 Par mi cel ost funt mil grailles suner;

186

Franc desherbergent, funt lur sumers trosser.
Vers dulce France tuit sunt achiminez.   AOI.

55

Carles li magnes ad Espaigne guastede,
Les castels pris, les citez violees;
Ço dit li reis que sa guere out finee.   705
Vers dulce France chevalchet l'emperere.
Li quens Rollant ad l'enseigne fermee,
En sum un tertre cuntre le ciel levee.
Franc se herbergent par tute la cuntree;
Paien chevalchent par cez greignurs valees,   710
Halbercs vestuz e . . .
Healmes lacez e ceintes lur espees,
Escuz as cols e lances adubees.
En un bruill par sum les puis remestrent;
·iiii·c· milie atendent l'ajurnee.   715
Deus, quel dulur que li Franceis nel sevent!   AOI.

56

Tresvait le jur, la noit est aserie.
Carles se dort, li empereres riches;
Sunjat qu'il eret as greignurs porz de Sizer,
Entre ses poinz teneit sa hanste fraisnine.   720
Guenes il quens l'ad sur lui saisie;
Par tel aïr l'at entrussee e brandie
Qu'envers le cel en volent les escicles.
Carles se dort, qu'il ne s'esveillet mie.

57

Aprés iceste altre avisiun sunjat,   725
Qu'il ert en France, a sa capele ad Ais.
El destre braz li morst uns vers si mals;
Devers Ardene vit venir uns leuparz,
Sun cors demenie mult fierement asalt.

730 D'enz de la sale uns veltres avalat
Que vint a Carles les galops e les salz.
La destre oreille al premer ver trenchat;
Ireement se cumbat al lepart.
Dient Franceis que grant bataille i ad;
735 Il ne sevent li quels d'els la veintrat.
Carles se dort, mie ne s'esveillat.   AOI.

58

Tresvait la noit e apert la clere albe.
Par mi cel host sunent . . . graisles;
Li empereres mult fierement chevalchet.
740 'Seignurs barons,' dist li empere Carles,
'Veez les porz e les destreiz passages;
Kar me jugez ki ert en la rereguarde.'
Guenes respunt: 'Rollant, cist miens fillastre;
N'avez baron de si grant vasselage.'
745 Quant l'ot li reis, fierement le reguardet,
Si li ad dit: 'Vos estes vifs diables;
El cors vos est entree mortel rage.
E ki serat devant mei en l'ansguarde?'
Guenes respunt: 'Oger de Denemarche;
750 N'avez barun ki mielz de lui la facet.'

59

Li quens Rollant, quant il s'oït juger,   AOI.
Dunc ad parléd a lei de chevaler:
'Sire parastre, mult vos dei aveir cher;
La rereguarde avez sur mei jugiét.
755 N'i perdrat Carles, li reis ki France tient,
Men escïentre palefreid ne destrer,
Ne mul ne mule que deiet chevalcher,
Ne n'i perdrat ne runcin ne sumer
Que as espees ne seit einz eslegiét.'
760 Guenes respunt: 'Veir dites, jol sai bien.'   AOI.

60

Quant ot Rollant qu'il ert en la rereguarde,
Ireement parlat a sun parastre:
'Ahi culvert, malvais hom de put aire,
Quias le guant me caïst en la place,
Cume fist a tei le bastun devant Carle?'   AOI.   765

61

'Dreiz emperere,' dist Rollant le barun,
'Dunez mei l'arc que vos tenez el poign;
Men escïentre nel me reproverunt
Que il me chedet, cum fist a Guenelun
De sa main destre, quant reçut le bastun.'   770
Li empereres en tint sun chef enbrunc,
Si duist sa barbe a detoerst sun gernun,
Ne poet müer que des oilz ne plurt.

62

Anprés iço i est Neimes venud;
Meillor vassal n'out en la curt de lui,   775
E dist al rei: 'Ben l'avez entendut,
Li quens Rollant il est mult irascut;
La rereguarde est jugee sur lui,
N'avez baron ki jamais la remut;
Dunez li l'arc que vos avez tendut,   780
Si li truvez ki tresbien li aiut.'
Li reis li dunet e Rollant l'a reçut.

63

Li empereres apelet ses niés Rollant:
'Bel sire niés, or savez veirement
Demi mun host vos lerrai en present.   785
Retenez les, ço est vostre salvement.'
Ço dit li quens: 'Jo n'en ferai nïent;
Deus me cunfunde, se la geste en desment.

·xx· milie Francs retrendrai ben vaillanz;
790 Passez les porz trestut soürement.
Ja mar crendrez nul hume a mun vivant!'

64

Li quens Rollant est muntét el destrer. AOI.
Cuntre lui vient sis cumpainz Oliver;
Vint i Gerins e li proz quens Gerers
795 E vint i Otes, si i vint Berengers
E vint i Astors e Anseïs li fiers;
Vint i Gerart de Rossillon li veillz,
Venuz i est li riches dux Gaifiers.
Dist l'arcevesque: 'Jo irai par mun chef.'
800 'E jo od vos,' ço dist li quens Gualters,
'Hom sui Rollant, jo ne li dei faillir.'
Entr'els eslisent ·xx· milie chevalers. AOI.

65

Li quens Rollant Gualter del Hum apelet:
'Pernez mil Francs de France nostre tere,
805 Si purpernez les destreiz e les tertres,
Que l'emperere nis un des soens n'i perdet.' AOI.
Respunt Gualter: 'Pur vos le dei ben faire.'
Od mil Franceis de France, la lur tere,
Gualter desrenget les destreiz e les tertres;
810 N'en descendrat pur malvaises nuveles
Enceis qu'en seient ·vii·c· espees traites.
Reis Almaris del regne de Belferne
Une bataille lur livrat le jur pesme.

66

Halt sunt li pui e li val tenebrus,
815 Les roches bises, les destreiz merveillus.
Le jur passerent Franceis a grant dulur,
De ·xv·liues en ot hom la rimur.

Puis que il venent a la tere majur,
Virent Guascuigne, la tere lur seignur.
Dunc lur remembret des fius e des honurs   820
E des pulceles e des gentilz oixurs;
Cel nen i ad ki de pitét ne plurt.
Sur tuz les altres est Carles anguissus;
As porz d'Espaigne ad lessét sun nevold,
Pitét l'en prent, ne poet müer n'en plurt.   AOI.   825

Oliver v. Roland

79
Paien s'adubent des osbercs sarazineis,
Tuit li plusur en sunt dublez en treis.   995
Lacent lor elmes mult bons sarraguzeis,
Ceignent espees de l'acer vianeis;
Escuz unt genz, espiez valentineis
E gunfanuns blancs e blois e vermeilz.
Laissent les muls e tuz les palefreiz;   1000
Es destrers muntent, si chevalchent estreiz.
Clers fut li jurz e bels fut li soleilz;
N'unt guarnement que tut ne reflambeit.
Sunent mil grailles por ço que plus bel seit;
Granz est la noise, si l'oïrent Franceis.   1005
Dist Oliver: 'Sire cumpainz, ce crei,
De Sarrazins purum bataille aveir.'
Respont Rollant: 'E Deus la nus otreit!
Ben devuns ci estre pur nostre rei;
Pur sun seignor deit hom susfrir destreiz   1010
E endurer e granz chalz e granz freiz,
Sin deit hom perdre e del quir e del peil.
Or guart chascuns que granz colps i empleit,
Que malvaise cançun de nus chantét ne seit.
Paien unt tort e chrestïens unt dreit;   1015
Malvaise essample n'en serat ja de mei.'   AOI.

191

80

Oliver est desur un pui halçur;
Guardet sur destre par mi un val herbus,
Si veit venir cele gent paienur,
1020 Sin apelat Rollant sun cumpaignun:
'Devers Espaigne vei venir tel brunur,
Tanz blancs osbercs, tanz elmes flambïus;
Icist ferunt nos Franceis grant irur.
Guenes le sout, li fel, li traïtur,
1025 Ki nus jugat devant l'empereür.'
'Tais, Oliver,' li quens Rollant respunt;
'Mis parrastre est, ne voeill que mot en suns.'

81

Oliver est desur un pui muntét;
Or veit il ben d'Espaigne le regnét
1030 E Sarrazins ki tant sunt asemblez.
Luisent cil elme ki ad or sunt gemmez
E cil escuz e cil osbercs safrez
E cil espiez, cil gunfanun fermez.
Sul les escheles ne poet il acunter,
1035 Tant en i ad que mesure n'en set.
E lui meïsme en est mult esguarét;
Cum il einz pout, del pui est avalét.
Vint as Franceis, tut lur ad acuntét.

82

Dist Oliver: 'Jo ai paiens veüz;
1040 Unc mais nuls hom en tere n'en vit plus.
Cil devant sunt ·c· milie ad escuz,
Helmes laciez e blancs osbercs vestuz,
Dreites cez hanstes, luisent cil espiét brun.
Bataille avrez, unches mais tel ne fut.
1045 Seignurs Franceis, de Deu aiez vertut;
El camp estez, que ne seium vencuz.'
Dient Franceis: 'Dehét ait ki s'en fuit;
Ja pur murir ne vus en faldrat uns.'   AOI.

83

Dist Oliver: 'Paien unt grant esforz;
De noz Franceis m'i semblet aveir mult poi.   1050
Cumpaign Rollant, kar sunez vostre corn,
Si l'orrat Carles, si returnerat l'ost.'
Respunt Rollant: 'Jo fereie que fols;
En dulce France en perdreie mun los.
Sempres ferrai de Durendal granz colps;   1055
Sanglant en ert li branz entresqu'a l'or.
Felun paien mar i vindrent as porz;
Jo vos plevis, tuz sunt jugez a mort.'   AOI.

84

'Cumpainz Rollant, l'olifan car sunez,
Si l'orrat Carles, ferat l'ost returner,   1060
Succurrat nos li reis od sun barnét.'
Respont Rollant: 'Ne placet Damnedeu
Que mi parent pur mei seient blasmét
Ne France dulce ja cheet en viltét.
Einz i ferrai de Durendal asez,   1065
Ma bone espee, que ai ceint al costét;
Tut en verrez le brant ensanglentét.
Felun paien mar i sunt asemblez;
Jo vos plevis, tuz sunt a mort livrez.'   AOI.

85

'Cumpainz Rollant, sunez vostre olifan,   1070
Si l'orrat Carles, ki est as porz passant.
Je vos plevis, ja returnerunt Franc.'
'Ne placet Deu,' ço li respunt Rollant,
'Que ço seit dit de nul hume vivant
Ne pur paien que ja seie cornant;   1075
Ja n'en avrunt reproece mi parent.
Quant jo serai en la bataille grant
E jo ferrai e mil colps e ·vii· cenz,
De Durendal verrez l'acer sanglent.

1080 Franceis sunt bon, si ferrunt vassalment;
Ja cil d'Espaigne n'avrunt de mort guarant.'

86

Dist Oliver: 'D'iço ne sai jo blasme;
Jo ai veüt les Sarrazins d'Espaigne.
Cuverz en sunt li val e les muntaignes
1085 E li lariz e trestutes les plaignes.
Granz sunt les oz de cele gent estrange;
Nus i avum mult petite cumpaigne.'
Respunt Rollant: 'Mis talenz en engraigne;
Ne placet Damnedeu ne ses angles
1090 Que ja pur mei perdet sa valur France.
Melz voeill murir que huntage me venget;
Pur ben ferir l'emperere plus nos aimet.'

87

Rollant est proz e Oliver est sage;
Ambedui unt meveillus vasselage.
1095 Puis que il sunt as chevals e as armes,
Ja pur murir n'eschiverunt bataille;
Bon sunt li cunte e lur paroles haltes.
Felun paien par grant irur chevalchent.
Dist Oliver: 'Rollant, veez en alques;
1100 Cist nus sunt pres, mais trop nus est loinz Carles.
Vostre olifan suner vos nel deignastes;
Fust i li reis, n'i oüssum damage.
Guardez amunt devers les porz d'Espaigne,
Veeir poëz, dolente est la rereguarde;
1105 Ki ceste fait jamais n'en ferat altre.'
Respunt Rollant: 'Ne dites tel ultrage;
Mal seit del coer ki el piz se cuardet!
Nus remeindrum en estal en la place;
Par nos i ert e li colps e li caples.'   AOI.

The Battle

93

Li nies Marsilie, il ad a num Aelroth,
Tut premereins chevalchet devant l'ost.
De noz Franceis vait disant si mals moz: 1190
'Feluns Franceis, hoi justerez as noz;
Traït vos ad ki a guarder vos out.
Fols est li reis ki vos laissat as porz;
Enquoi perdrat France dulce sun los,
Charles li magnes le destre braz del cors!'   1195
Quant l'ot Rollant, Deus, si grant doel en out.
Sun cheval brochet, laiset curre a esforz;
Vait le ferir li quens quanque il pout.
L'escut li freint e l'osberc li desclot;
Trenchet le piz, si li briset les os,   1200
Tute l'eschine li desevret del dos.
Od sun espiét l'anme li getet fors;
Enpeint le ben, fait li brandir le cors,
Pleine sa hanste del cheval l'abat mort.
En dous meitiez li ad brisét le col;   1205
Ne leserat, ço dit, que n'i parolt:
'Ultre culvert, Carles n'est mie fol,
Ne traïsun unkes amer ne volt;
Il fist que proz qu'il nus laisad as porz,
Oi n'en perdrat France dulce sun los.   1210
Ferez i, Francs, nostre est li premers colps;
Nos avum dreit, mais cist glutun unt tort.'   AOI.

94

Un duc i est, si ad num Falsaron;
Icil ert frere al rei Marsiliun.
Il tint la tere Dathan e Abirun,   1215
Suz cel nen at plus encrisme felun.
Entre les dous oilz mult out large le front,
Grant demi pied mesurer i pout hom.
Asez ad doel quant vit mort sun nevold;

1220 Ist de la prese, si se met en bandun
E si escriet l'enseigne paienor,
Envers Franceis est mult cuntrarïus:
'Enquoi perdrat France dulce s'onur.'
Ot le Oliver, sin ad mult grant irur.

1225 Le cheval brochet des oriez esperuns;
Vait le ferir en guise de baron.
L'escut li freint e l'osberc li derumpt;
El cors li met les pans del gunfanun,
Pleine sa hanste l'abat mort des arçuns.

1230 Guardet a tere, veit gesir le glutun,
Si li ad dit par mult fiere raison:
'De voz manaces, culvert, jo n'ai essoign.
Ferez i, Francs, kar tresben les veintrum.'
Munjoie escriet, ço est l'enseigne Carlun.   AOI.

95
1235 Uns reis i est, si ad num Corsablix;
Barbarins est d'un estrange païs,
Si apelad les altres Sarrazins:
'Ceaste bataille ben la puum tenir,
Kar de Franceis i ad asez petit.

1240 Cels ki ci sunt devum aveir mult vil;
Ja pur Charles n'i ert un sul guarit.
Or est le jur qu'els estuvrat murir.'
Ben l'entendit li arcevesques Turpin;
Suz ciel n'at hume que tant voeillet haïr.

1245 Sun cheval brochet des esperuns d'or fin;
Par grant vertut si l'est alét ferir.
L'escut li freinst, l'osberc li descumfist;
Sun grant espiét par mi le cors li mist.
Empeint le ben, que mort le fait brandir,

1250 Pleine sa hanste l'abat mort el chemin.
Guardet arere, veit le glutun gesir;
Ne laisserat que n'i parolt, ço dit:
'Culvert paien, vos i avez mentit.
Carles, mi sire, nus est guarant tuz dis;

Nostre Franceis n'unt talent de fuïr. 1255
Voz cumpaignuns feruns trestuz restifs;
Nuveles vos di, mort vos estoet susfrir.
Ferez, Franceis, nul de vus ne s'ublit;
Cist premer colp est nostre, Deu mercit.'
Munjoie escriet por le camp retenir. 1260

96
E Gerins fiert Malprimis de Brigal;
Sis bons escuz un dener ne li valt.
Tute li freint la bucle de cristal;
L'une meitiét li turnet cuntreval.
L'osberc li rumpt entresque a la charn; 1265
Sun bon espiét enz el cors li enbat.
Li paiens chet cuntreval a un quat;
L'anme de lui en portet Sathanas. AOI.

Roland's Lament

140
Rollant reguardet es munz e es lariz;
De cels de France i veit tanz morz gesir,
E il les pluret cum chevaler gentill:
'Seignors barons, de vos ait Deus mercit.
Tutes voz anmes otreit il pareïs: 1855
En seintes flurs il les facet gesir.
Meillors vassals de vos unkes ne vi.
Si lungement tuz tens m'avez servit,
A oes Carlon si granz païs cunquis.
Li empereres tant mare vos nurrit! 1860
Tere de France, mult estes dulz païs,
Oi desertét a tant ruboste exill!
Barons franceis, pur mei vos vei murir;
Jo ne vos pois tenser ne guarantir.
Aït vos Deus ki unkes ne mentit; 1865
Oliver, frere, vos ne dei jo faillir,
De doel murrai, se altre ne m'i ocit.
Sire cumpainz, alum i referir.'

141

Li quens Rollant el champ est repairét;
1870 Tient Durendal, cume vassal i fiert,
Faldrun de Pui i ad par mi trenchét
E ·xxiiii· de tuz les melz preisez.
Jamais n'iert home, plus se voeillet venger.
Si cum li cerfs s'en vait devant les chiens,
1875 Devant Rollant si s'en fuient paiens.
Dist l'arcevesque: 'Asez le faites ben;
Itel valor deit aveir chevaler,
Ki armes portet e en bon cheval set.
En bataille deit estre forz e fiers,
1880 U altrement ne valt ·iiii· deners;
Einz deit monie estre en un de cez mustiers,
Si prierat tuz jurz por noz peccez.'
Respunt Rollant: 'Ferez, nes esparignez.'
A icest mot l'unt Francs recumencét;
1885 Mult grant damage i out de chrestïens.

The Death of Roland

168

Ço sent Rollant que la mort li est pres;
2260 Par les oreilles fors s'en ist li cervel.
De ses pers priet Deu ques apelt.
E pois de lui a l'angle Gabrïel.
Prist l'olifan, que reproce n'en ait,
E Durendal s'espee en l'altre main.
2265 Plus qu'arcbaleste ne poet traire un quarrel
Devers Espaigne en vait en un guarét;
Muntet sur un tertre desuz un arbre bel,
Quatre perruns i ad de marbre faiz.
Sur l'erbe verte si est caeit envers;
2270 La s'est pasmét, kar la mort li est pres.

169

Halt sunt li pui e mult halt les arbres.
Quatre perruns i ad luisant de marbre;
Sur l'erbe verte li quens Rollant se pasmet.
Uns Sarrazins tute veie l'esguardet,
Si se feinst mort, si gist entre les altres,   2275
Del sanc luat sun cors e sun visage.
Met sei en piez e de curre se hastet.
Bels fut e forz e de grant vasselage,
Par sun orgoill cumencet mortel rage.
Rollant saisit e sun cors e ses armes   2280
E dist un mot: 'Vencut est li niés Carles;
Iceste espee porterai en Arabe.'
En cel tirer li quens s'aperçut alques.

170

Ço sent Rollant que s'espee li tolt.
Uvrit les oilz, si li ad dit un mot: 2285
'Men escïentre tu n'ies mie des noz.'
Tient l'olifan, que unkes perdre ne volt,
Sil fiert en l'elme ki gemmét fut a or.
Fruisset l'acer e la teste e les os;
Amsdous les oilz del chef li ad mis fors,   2290
Jus a ses piez si l'ad tresturnét mort.
Aprés li dit: 'Culvert paien, cum fus unkes si os
Que me saisis, ne a dreit ne a tort?
Ne l'orrat hume ne t'en tienget por fol;
Fenduz en est mis olifans el gros,   2295
Caiuz en est li cristals e li ors.'

171

Ço sent Rollant la veüe ad perdue.
Met sei sur piez, quanqu'il poet s'esvertuet;
En sun visage sa culur ad perdue.
Dedevant lui ad une perre byse;   2300
·x· colps i fiert par doel e par rancune.
Cruist li acers, ne freint ne n'esgruignet:

'E,' dist li quens, 'seinte Marie, aiue!
E, Durendal bone, si mare fustes!
2305 Quant jo mei perd, de vos nen ai mais cure.
Tantes batailles en camp en ai vencues
E tantes teres larges escumbatues,
Que Carles tient, ki la barbe ad canue.
Ne vos ait hume ki pur altre fuiet;
2310 Mult bon vassal vos ad lung tens tenue.
Jamais n'ert tel en France l'asolue.'

172

Rollant ferit el perrun de sardonie;
Cruist li acers, ne briset ne n'esgrunie.
Quant il ço vit que n'en pout mie freindre,
2315 A sei meïsme la cumencet a pleindre:
'E, Durendal, cum es bele e clere e blanche!
Cuntre soleill si luises e reflambes!
Carles esteit es vals de Moriane,
Quant Deus del cel li mandat par sun angle
2320 Qu'il te dunast a un cunte cataignie;
Dunc la me ceinst li gentilz reis, li magnes.
Jo l'en cunquis e Anjou e Bretaigne,
Si l'en cunquis e Peitou e le Maine;
Jo l'en cunquis Normendie la franche,
2325 Si l'en cunquis Provence e Equitaigne
E Lumbardie e trestute Romaine.
Jo l'en cunquis Baiver e tute Flandres
E Burguigne e trestute Puillanie,
Costentinnoble, dunt il out la fiance,
2330 E en Saisonie fait il ço qu'il demandet,
Jo l'en cunquis e Escoce e Irlande
E Engletere, que il teneit sa cambre.
Cunquis l'en ai païs e teres tantes,
Que Carles tient, ki ad la barbe blanche.
2335 Pur ceste espee ai dulor e pesance;
Mielz voeill murir qu'entre paiens remaigne.
Deus, pere, n'en laiser hunir France!'

173

Rollant ferit en une perre bise;
Plus en abat que jo ne vos sai dire.
L'espee cruist, ne fruisset ne ne brise; 2340
Cuntre ciel amunt est resortie.
Quant veit li quens que ne la freindrat mie,
Mult dulcement la pleinst a sei meïsme:
'E, Durendal, cum es bele e seintisme!
En l'oriét punt asez i ad reliques: 2345
La dent seint Perre e del sanc seint Basilie
E des chevels mun seignor seint Denise;
Del vestement i ad seinte Marie.
Il nen est dreiz que paiens te baillisent;
De chrestïens devez estre servie. 2350
Ne vos ait hume ki facet cuardie.
Mult larges teres de vus avrai conquises;
Carles les tent, ki la barbe ad flurie,
E li empereres en est ber e riches.'

174

Ço sent Rollant que la mort le tresprent; 2355
Devers la teste sur le quer li descent.
Desuz un pin i est alét curant;
Sur l'erbe verte s'i est culchét adenz.
Desuz lui met s'espee e l'olifan;
Turnat sa teste vers la paiene gent. 2360
Pur ço l'at fait que il voelt veirement
Que Carles diet e trestute sa gent,
Li gentilz quens, qu'il fut mort cunquerant.
Cleimet sa culpe e menut e suvent;
Pur ses pecchez Deu en puroffrid lo guant. AOI. 2365

175

Ço sent Rollant de sun tens n'i ad plus;
Devers Espaigne est en un pui agut,
A l'une main si ad sun piz batud:

'Deus, meie culpe vers les tues vertuz,
2370 De mes pecchez, des granz e des menuz,
Que jo ai fait des l'ure que nez fui,
Tresqu'a cest jur que ci sui consoüt.'
Sun destre guant en ad vers Deu tendut;
Angles del ciel i descendent a lui.   AOI.

176

2375 Li quens Rollant se jut desuz un pin;
Envers Espaigne en ad turnét sun vis.
De plusurs choses a remembrer li prist:
De tantes teres cum li bers cunquist,
De dulce France, des humes de sun lign,
2380 De Carlemagne, sun seignor kil nurrit.
Ne poet müer n'en plurt e ne suspirt,
Mais lui meïsme ne volt mettre en ubli.
Cleimet sa culpe, si priet Deu mercit:
'Veire Patene, ki unkes ne mentis,
2385 Seint Lazaron de mort resurrexis
E Daniël des leons guaresis,
Guaris de mei l'anme de tuz perilz,
Pur les pecchez que en ma vie fis.
Sun destre guant a Deu en puroffrit;
2390 Seint Gabriël de sa main l'ad pris.
Desur sun braz teneit le chef enclin;
Juntes ses mains est alét a sa fin.
Deus tramist sun angle Cherubin,
Ensembl'od li seint Michel del Peril;
2395 Ensembl'od els sent Gabriël i vint.
L'anme del cunte portent en pareis.

The Trial of Ganelon

278

3750 'Seignors barons,' dist Carlemagnes li reis,
'De Guenelun car me jugez le dreit.
Il fut en l'ost tresque en Espaigne od mei,

Si me tolit ·xx· milie de mes Franceis
E mun nevold, que ja mais ne verreiz,
E Oliver, li proz e li curteis; 3755
Les ·xii· pers ad traït por aveir.'
Dist Guenelon: 'Fel seie, se jol ceil.
Rollanz me forfist en or e en aveir,
Pur que jo quis sa mort e sun destreit;
Mais traïsun nule nen i otrei.' 3760
Respundent Franc: 'Ore en tendrum cunseill.'

279

Devant le rei la s'estut Guenelun.
Cors ad gaillard, el vis gente color;
S'il fust leials, ben resemblast barun.
Veit cels de France e tuz les jugeürs, 3765
De ses parenz ·xxx· ki od lui sunt;
Puis s'escriat haltement a grant voeiz:
'Por amor Deu, car m'entendez, barons!
Seignors, jo fui en l'ost avoec l'empereür;
Serveie le par feid e par amur. 3770
Rollant sis niés me coillit en haür,
Si me jugat a mort e a dulur.
Message fui al rei Marsiliun;
Par mun saveir vinc jo a guarisun.
Jo desfiai Rollant le poigneor 3775
E Oliver e tuiz lur cumpaignun.
Carles l'oïd e si nobilie baron;
Vengét m'en sui, mais n'i ad traïsun.'
Respundent Francs: 'A conseill en irums.'

280

Quant Guenes veit que ses granz plaiz cumencet, 3780
De ses parenz ensemble od li out trente.
Un en i ad a qui li altre entendent:
Ço est Pinabel del Castel de Sorence.
Ben set parler e dreite raisun rendre;
Vassals est bons por ses armes defendre. AOI. 3785

281

Ço li dist Guenes: 'En vos . . . ami . . .
Getez mei hoi de mort e de calenge.'
Dist Pinabel: 'Vos serez guarit sempres.
N'i ad Frances ki vos juget a pendre,
3790 U l'emperere les noz dous cors en asemblet,
Al brant d'acer que jo ne l'en desmente.'
Guenes li quens a ses piez se presente.

282

Bavier e Saisnes sunt alét a conseill
E Peitevin e Norman e Franceis.
3795 Asez i ad Alemans e Tiedeis;
Icels d'Alverne i sunt li plus curteis.
Pur Pinabel se cuntienent plus quei.
Dist l'un a l'altre: 'Bien fait a remaneir.
Laisum le plait e si preium le rei
3800 Que Guenelun cleimt quite ceste feiz;
Puis si li servet par amur e par feid.
Morz est Rollant, ja mais nel revereiz;
N'ert recuvrét por or ne por aveir.
Mult sereit fols ki ja se cumbatreit.'
3805 Nen i ad celoi nel graant e otreit,
Fors sul Tierri, le frere dam Geifreit.   AOI.

283

A Charlemagne repairent si barun.
Dient al rei: 'Sire, nus vos prïum
Que clamez quite le cunte Guenelun;
3810 Puis si vos servet par feid e par amor.
Vivre le laisez, car mult est gentilz hoem.
Ja por murir n'en ert veüd cist barun,
Ne por aveir ja nel recuverum.'
Ço dist li reis: 'Vos estes mi felun.'   AOI.

284

Quant Carles veit que tuz li sunt faillid,   3815
Mult l'enbrunchit e la chere e le vis;
Al doel qu'il ad si se cleimet caitifs.
Ais li devant uns chevalers, Tierris,
Frere Gefrei, a un duc angevin.
Heingre out le cors e graisle e eschewid,   3820
Neirs les chevels e alques bruns li vis;
N'est gueres granz, ne trop nen est petiz.
Curteisement a l'emperere ad dit:
'Bels sire reis, ne vous dementez si;
Ja savez vos que mult vos ai servit,   3825
Par anceisurs dei jo tel plait tenir.
Que que Rollant a Guenelun forsfesist,
Vostre servise l'en doüst bien guarir.
Guenes est fels d'iço qu'il le traït;
Vers vos s'en est parjurez e malmis.   3830
Pur ço le juz jo a pendre e a murir
E sun cors metre . . .
Si cume fel ki felonie fist.
Se or ad parent ki m'en voeille desmentir,
A ceste espee que jo ai ceinte ici   3835
Mun jugement voel sempres guarantir.'
Respundent Franc: 'Or avez vos ben dit.'

285

Devant lu rei est venuz Pinabel;
Granz est e forz e vassals e isnel.
Qu'il fiert a colp de sun tens n'i ad mais.   3840
E dist al rei: 'Sire, vostre est li plaiz;
Car cumandez que tel noise n'i ait.
Ci vei Tierri, ki jugement ad fait,
Jo si li fals, od lui m'en cumbatrai.'
Met li el poign de cerf le destre guant.   3845
Dist li empereres: 'Bons pleges en demant.'
·xxx· parenz l'i plevissent leial.
Ço dist li reis: 'E jol vos recrerai.'
Fait cels guarder tresque li dreiz en serat.   AOI.

286

3850 Quant veit Tierri qu'or en ert la bataille,
Sun destre guant en ad presentét Carle.
Li emperere l'i recreit par hostage,
Puis fait porter ·iiii· bancs en la place;
La vunt sedeir cil ki s deivent cumbatre.
3855 Ben sunt malez par jugement des altres,
Sil purparlat Oger de Denemarche;
E puis demandent lur chevals e lur armes.

287

Puis que il sunt a bataille jugez,   AOI.
Ben sunt cunfés e asols e seignez.
3860 Oënt lur messes e sunt acuminjez,
Mult granz offrendes metent par cez musters.
Devant Carlun andui sunt repairez;
Lur esperuns unt en lor piez calcez,
Vestent osberc blancs e forz e legers,
3865 Lur helmes clers unt fermez en lor chefs,
Ceinent espees enheldees d'or mier,
En lur cols pendent lur escuz de quarters,
En lur puinz destres unt lur trenchanz espiez.
Puis sunt muntez en lur curanz destrers;
3870 Idunc plurerent ·c· milie chevalers
Qui pur Rollant de Tierri unt pitiét.
Deus set asez cument la fins en ert.

288

Dedesuz Ais est la pree mult large;
Des dous baruns justee est la bataille.
3875 Cil sunt produme e de grant vasselage
E lur chevals sunt curanz e aates;
Brochent les bien, tutes les resnes lasquent.
Par grant vertut vait ferir l'uns li altre;
Tuz lur escuz i fruissent e esquassent,
3880 Lur osbercs rumpent e lur cengles depiecent,

Les alves turnent, les seles cheent a tere.
·c· milie humes i plurent kis esguardent.

289

A tere sunt ambdui li chevaler;   AOI.
Isnelement se drecent sur lur piez.
Pinabels est forz e isnels e legers;   3885
Li uns requiert l'altre, n'unt mie des destrers.
De cez espees enheldees d'or mer
Fierent e caplent sur cez helmes d'acer.
Granz sunt les colps as helmes detrencher;
Mult se dementent cil franceis chevaler.   3890
'E, Deus,' dist Carles, 'le dreit en esclargiez!'

290

Dist Pinabel: 'Tierri, car te recreiz.
Tes hom serai par amur e par feid,
A tun plaisir te durrai mun aveir;
Mais Guenelun fai acorder al rei.'   3895
Respont Tierri: 'Ja n'en tendrai cunseill,
Tut seie fel, se jo mie l'otrei.
Deus facet hoi entre nus dous le dreit.'   AOI.

291

Ço dist Tierri: 'Pinabel, mult ies ber;
Granz ies e forz e tis cors ben mollez.   3900
De vasselage te conoissent ti per.
Ceste bataille, car la laisses ester;
A Carlemagne te ferai acorder.
De Guenelun justise ert faite tel;
Jamais n'ert jur que il n'en seit parlét.'   3905
Dist Pinabel: 'Ne placet Damnedeu;
Sustenir voeill trestut mun parentét.
N'en recrerrai pur nul hume mortel;
Mielz voeill murir que il me seit reprovét.'

3910 De lur espees cumencent a capler
Desur cez helmes, ki sunt a or gemez;
Cuntre le ciel en volet li fous tuz clers.
Il ne poet estre qu'il seient desevrez;
Seinz hume mort ne poet estre afinét.   AOI.

                            292
3915 Mult par est proz Pinabel de Sorence,
Si fiert Tierri sur l'elme de Provence;
Salt en li fous que l'erbe en fait esprendre.
Del brant d'acer la mure li presentet,
Desur le frunt . . .
3920 Em mi le vis li ad faite descendre.
La destre joe en ad tute sanglente;
L'osberc desclos josque par sum le ventre.
Deus le guarit que mort ne l'acraventet.   AOI.

                            293
     Ço veit Tierris que el vis est ferut;
3925 Li sancs tuz clers en chiet el pred herbus.
Fiert Pinabel sur l'elme d'acer brun,
Jusqu'al nasel li ad frait e fendut;
Del chef li ad le cervel espandut,
Brandit sun colp si l'ad mort abatut.
3930 A icest colp est li esturs vencut.
Escrient Franc: 'Deus i ad fait vertut;
Asez est dreiz que Guenes seit pendut
E si parent ki plaidét unt pur lui.'   AOI.

                            294
     Quant Tierris ad vencue sa bataille,
3935 Venuz i est li emperere Carles,
Ensembl'od lui de ses baruns quarante.
Naimes li dux, Oger de Danemarche,
Geifrei d'Anjou e Willalme de Blaive.

Li reis ad pris Tierri entre sa brace;
Tert lui le vis od ses granz pels de martre, 3940
Celes met jus, puis li afublent altres.
Mult suavet le chevaler desarment;
Fait le monter en une mule d'Arabe.
Repairet s'en a joie e a barnage;
Vienent ad Ais, descendent en la place. 3945
Des ore cumencet l'ocisïun des altres.

295

Carles apelet ses cuntes e ses dux:
'Que me loëz de cels qu'ai retenuz?
Pur Guenelun erent a plait venuz,
Pur Pinabel en ostage renduz.' 3950
Respundent Franc: 'Ja mar en vivrat uns.'
Li reis cumandet un soen veier, Basbrun:
'Va, sis pent tuz a l'arbre de mal fust;
Par ceste barbe dunt li peil sunt canuz,
Se uns escapet, morz ies e cunfunduz.' 3955
Cil li respunt: 'Qu'en fereie joe plus?'
Od ·c· serjanz par force les cunduit;
·xxx· en i ad d'icels ki sunt pendut.
Ki hume traïst sei ocit e altroi.   AOI.

296

Puis sunt turnét Bavier e Aleman 3960
E Peitevin e Bretun e Norman.
Sor tuit li altre l'unt otriét li Franc
Que Guenes moerget par merveillus ahan.
Quatre destrers funt amener avant,
Puis si li lient e les piez e les mains. 3965
Li cheval sunt orgoillus e curant;
Quatre serjanz les acoeillent devant.
Devers un' ewe ki est en mi un camp
Guenes est turnét a perdicïun grant.
Trestuit si nerf mult li sunt estendant 3970

209

E tuit li membre de sun cors derumpant;
Sur l'erbe verte en espant li cler sanc.
Guenes est mort cume fel recreant.
Hom ki traïst altre nen est dreiz qu'il s'en vant.

297

3975 Quant li empereres ad faite sa venjance,
Sin apelat ses evesques de France,
Cels de Baviere e icels d'Alemaigne:
'En ma maisun ad une caitive franche;
Tant ad oït e sermuns e essamples
3980 Creire voelt Deu, chrestïentét demandet.
Baptizez la, pur quei Deus en ait l'anme.'
Cil li respundent: 'Or seit fait par marrenes,
Asez cruiz e linees dames.'
As bainz ad Ais mult sunt granz les cumpaignes;
3985 La baptizent la reïne d'Espaigne.
Truvét li unt le num de Juliane;
Chrestïene est par veire conoisance.

298

Quant l'emperere ad faite sa justise
E esclargiez est la sue grant ire,
3990 En Bramidonie ad chrestïentét mise.
Passet li jurz, la nuit est aserie,
Culcez s'est li reis en sa cambre voltice.
Seint Gabrïel de part Deu li vint dire:
'Carles, sumun les oz de tun emperie.
3995 Par force iras en la tere de Bire,
Reis Vivïen si succuras en Imphe,
A la citét que paien unt asise;
Li chrestïen te recleiment e crient.'
Li emperere n'i volsist aler mie;
4000 'Deus,' dist li reis, 'si penuse est ma vie!'
Pluret des oilz, sa barbe blanche tiret.
Ci falt la geste que Turoldus declinet.

Index of Proper Names

Manuscript forms, if different from those used in the translation, are given in brackets. For further information and discussion of the problems relating to the identification of proper names see Bédier, *Commentaires*, pp. 505–22, Boissonnade, Duggan, *Concordance*, pp. 392–420, *A Guide to Studies on the Chanson de Roland*, pp. 56–60, and Mireaux.

211

Armenians (*Ermines*), 3227.
Astor, 796. A Frank.
Astramariz, 1304. See Estramariz.
Astrimoines (*Astrimonies*), 3258. A Saracen tribe.
Atton (*Atuin*), 2187. A Frank.
Aude (*Alde*), 1720, 3708, 3717, 3723. Oliver's sister.
Austorie, 1625. A Frankish duke.
Auvergne (*Alvernene*), 3062, 3796.
Avars (*Avers*), 3242. A Saracen tribe of Tartar origin.

Babylon (*Babilonie*), 2614. Old Cairo in Egypt.
Balaguer (*Balaguet, Balaguez, Balasgued*), 63, 200, 894. Stronghold in Catalonia, east of Saragossa.
Baldise the Long, 3255. A Saracen town.
Baldwin (*Baldewin*), 314, 363. Ganelon's son.
Balide, 3230. A Saracen town.
Baligant, 2614, 2622, 2654, 2725, etc. Emir of Babylon, Marsile's lord.
Barbamusche, 1534. Climborin's horse.
Basan (*Basan, Basant*), 208, 330, 490. A Frankish count.
Basbrun, 3952. Charlemagne's provost-marshal.
Bascle, 3474. A Saracen town.
Basile (*Basilie, Basilies*), 208, 330, 490. A Frankish count, brother of Basan.
Bavaria (*Bavier, Baivere, Baiver*), 2327, 3028, 3977.
Bavarian (*Bavier, Baivers*), 3700, 3793, 3960.
Beaune (*Belne*), 1892. A town in Burgundy, S E of Dijon.
Belferne, 812. A Saracen kingdom.
Berber (adj. *barbarins*, 886), 886, 1236.
Berenger, 795, 1304, 1624, 2187, 2405. A Frank.
Besançon (*Besençun*), 1429.
Besgun, 1818. Charlemagne's head cook.
Bevon, 1891. A Frank.
Bire, 3995. Perhaps the fortress of Elbira, near Granada.
Blancandrin (*Blanchandrins*, 413), 23, 24, 47, 68, etc. The instigator of the pagan plot and Marsile's messenger to Charles.
Blaye (*Blaive*), 3689, 3938. Blaye-sur-Gironde (*Landes*), near Bordeaux.
Blos, 3224. A pagan people, perhaps the Cumans or the Polovzians.
Bordeaux (*Burdel, Burdele, Burdeles*), 1289, 1389, 3684.
Bramimonde (*Bramimunde, Bramidonie*), 634, 2576, 2595, 2714, 2734, 2822, 3636, 3655, 3680. Marsile's queen.
Breton (*Bretun, Bretuns*), 3052, 3702, 3961.
Brigal, 1261, Brigant, 889. Presumably the same place, perhaps Berbegal in Aragon.
Brittany (*Bretaigne*), 2322.
Bruise, 3245. A Saracen country, perhaps Brusa in Bithynia.
Bruns, 3225. A pagan people.
Bulgars (*Bugre*), 2922.
Burdel, 1388. A Saracen (see note to v. 1389).
Burgundians (*Borguignuns*), 3701.
Burgundy (*Borgoigne, Burguigne*), 2328, 3077.
Butentrot, 3220. Perhaps Butentrot in Cappadocia or Butintro in Epirus.

INDEX OF PROPER NAMES

Calabria (*Calabre*), 371.
Califerne, 2924. A Saracen town or country.
Canaanites (*Canelius*), 3238, 3269. A name for the Saracens.
Canabeus, 3312, 3429, 3499. Baligant's brother.
Cappadocia (*Capadoce*), 1614. Ancient province in Asia Minor.
Capuel, 1614. King of Cappadocia.
Carcassonne (*Carcasonie*), 385. French town (Aude).
Carthage (*Karthagene*), 1915.
Castel de Sorence, see Sorence.
Castel de Valfunde, 23. Saracen location, Blancandrin's home.
Cazmarines, 956. Perhaps Camariñas in Galicia.
Charlemagne (*Carlemagne, Carlemagnes, Karlemagne*), 70, 81, etc. The Frankish
    emperor.
Charles (*Carles, Karle, Carle, Charle, Carlun, Carlon, Charlun, Karlon*), 1, 16, 28,
    etc. Charlemagne.
Cheriant, 3208. Saracen location, perhaps Kairouan in Tunisia.
Chernubles, 975, 984, 1310, 1325. A Saracen.
Cherubin, 2393. The angel Cherubin.
Cize, pass of (*Sirie, Sizer*), 583, 719, 2939. The Col de Cize, valley on the north slope
    of the Pyrenees.
Clarbone, 3259. A Saracen location.
Clarien, 2670, 2724, 2771, 2790. A Saracen, Baligant's messenger.
Clarifan, 2670. A Saracen, brother of Clarien, Baligant's messenger.
Clarin, 63. A Saracen.
Clavers, 3245. A pagan people.
Climborin (*Climorins*), 627, 1528. A Saracen.
Commibles, 198. Portuguese or Spanish town.
Constantinople (*Costentinnoble*), 2329.
Cordoba (*Cordre*), 71, 97.
Corsablix, 1235. Saracen king.
Corsalis, 885. Presumably same as Corsablix.

Dane (*Daneis*), see Ogier (the Dane).
Daniel, 2386, 3104. Biblical prophet.
Dapamort, 3205, 3216. King of Lycia.
Dathan, 1215. Biblical character (see Numbers, chapter 16).
Denmark (*Danemarche, Denemerche*), 749, 1489, 3937.
Dijon (*Digun*), 1892. French town (Côte-d'Or).
Droun, 2048. A Frank, uncle of Gautier del Hum.
Durendal, 926, 988, 1065, 1079, etc. Roland's sword.
Durestant, 870. A Spanish location.

Ebro (*Sebre*), 2465, 2642, 2728, 2758, 2798. River in Spain (rises in the Cantabrian
    Mountains and flows S E to the Mediterranean).
Enfruns, 3518. A pagan people.
Engeler, 1289, 1537, 1546. A Frank.
England (*Engletere*), 372, 2332.
Escababi, 1555. A Saracen.
Escremiz, 931, 1291. A Saracen.
Espaneliz, 2648. A Saracen.

Malpalin, 2995. A Saracen.
Malpramis, 3176, 3184, 3200, 3201, 3369, 3421, 3498. Baligant's son.
Malpreis, 3285. A Saracen location, presumably same as Malprose.
Malprimis, 889, 1261. A Saracen.
Malprose, 3253. A Saracen location (see Malpreis).
Malquiant, 1594. A Saracen, son of King Malcuid.
Maltet, 3152. Baligant's spear.
Maltraien, 2671. A Saracen king.
Malun, 1353. A Saracen.
Marbrise, 2641. A place which is passed by Baligant's fleet.
Marbrose, 2641. As Marbrise.
Marcule, 3156. A Saracen.
Marganice, 1914, 1943, 1954. Marsile's uncle.
Margariz, 955, 1310, 1311. A Saracen count.
Marmorie, 1615. Grandonie's horse.
Marose, 3257. Saracen location.
Marsile (*Marcilie, Marsille, Marsilies, Marsilun, Marsiliuns*), 7, 10, 62, 78, 89, etc.,
  Saracen king of Spain.
Marsonne (*Marsune*), 2994. Unidentified place.
Mary, Virgin, 1473, 2303, 2348, 2938.
Matthew (*Maheu*), 66. A Saracen, uncle of Machiner.
Maurienne, Vales of (*Vals de Moriane*), 2318. A high Alpine valley in S E France.
Mayence (*Maience*), 3008. Port in West Germany (Mainz).
Michaelmas (*feste seint Michel*), 37, 53. See Saint Michael.
Milceni (*Micenes*), 3221. A Slavonic people.
Milon (*Milun*), 173, 2433, 2971. A Frankish count.
Monjoie (*Munjoie*), 1182, 1234, 1260, 1350, etc. The battle-cry of Charlemagne,
  'Mountjoy'.
Moors (*Mors*), 3227.
Moriane, 909. Perhaps Moriana on the Ebro.
Muhammad (*Mahum, Mahumet*), 8, 416, 611, 853, 868, etc. Saracen god (see Apollo
  and Tervagant).
Munigre, 975. Perhaps Monegrillo on the Ebro or Los Monigros, E of Saragossa.
Murgleis (*Murglies*), 346, 607. Ganelon's sword.

Naimes (*Neimes, Naimon, Naimun*), 230, 246, 673, 831, etc. Frankish duke and
  Charlemagne's counsellor.
Narbonne (*Nerbone*), 2995, 3683. French city (Aude). May be confused in v. 3683
  with Arbonne near Biarritz.
Nevelon, 3057. A Frankish count.
Nigres, 3229. A pagan people.
Niniveh (*Niniven*), 3103. Capital of Assyria.
Noples, 198, 1775. City in Spain, perhaps Napal in the diocese of Barbastro.
Normandy, 2324.
Normans, 3045, 3470, 3702, 3794, 3961.
Nubles, 3224. A pagan people.

Occian the Desert (*Occiant, Ociant*), 3246, 3286, 3474, 3517, 3526. A Saracen
  region.
Oedun, 3056. Lord of the Bretons.

INDEX OF PROPER NAMES

PENGUIN CLASSICS

GISLI SURSSON'S SAGA *AND* THE SAGA OF THE PEOPLE OF EYRI

'Fate must find someone to speak through. Whatever is meant to happen will happen'

Based on oral tales that originated from historical events in tenth-century Iceland, these two sagas follow the fate of a powerful Viking family across two generations, from its Norwegian ancestry through fierce battles to defend its honour. *Gisli Sursson's Saga* is a story of forbidden love and divided loyalties, in which the heroic Gisli vows to avenge the murder of his 'sworn brother' and sets in motion a chain of bloody events that culminate in tragedy. *The Saga of the People of Eyri* continues the story with Snorri, a cunning leader of the next generation, who uses his intellect to restore social order. Blending gripping narrative, humour, the supernatural and shrewd observation, these tales reveal the richness of the saga tradition and present a vivid record of a society moving from individualism to a Christian ethic of reconciliation and order.

These clear, contemporary translations are accompanied by an introduction giving historical and literary background to the sagas. This edition also includes appendices, maps, notes on the texts, a glossary and an index of characters.

Translated by Martin S. Regal and Judy Quinn
Edited with an introduction by Vésteinn Ólason

PENGUIN CLASSICS

THE NEW PENGUIN BOOK OF ROMANTIC POETRY

'And what if all of animated Nature
Be but organic harps, diversely framed'

The Romanticism that emerged after the American and French revolutions of 1776 and 1789 represented a new flowering of the imagination and the spirit, and a celebration of the soul of humanity with its capacity for love. This extraordinary collection sets the acknowledged genius of poems such as Blake's 'Tyger', Coleridge's 'Khubla Khan' and Shelley's 'Ozymandias' alongside verse from less familiar figures and women poets such as Charlotte Smith and Mary Robinson. We also see familiar poets in an unaccustomed light, as Blake, Wordsworth and Shelley demonstrate their comic skills, while Coleridge, Keats and Clare explore the Gothic and surreal.

This volume is arranged by theme and genre, revealing unexpected connections between the poets. In their introduction Jonathan and Jessica Wordsworth explore Romanticism as a way of responding to the world, and they begin each section with a helpful preface, notes and bibliography.

'An absolutely fascinating selection – notable for its women poets, its intriguing thematic categories and its helpful mini biographies' Richard Holmes

Edited with an introduction by Jonathan and Jessica Wordsworth read more 🄟

PENGUIN CLASSICS

LE MORTE D'ARTHUR, VOLUME 1
SIR THOMAS MALORY

'Well-nigh all the world holdeth with Arthur, for there is the flower of chivalry'

Le Morte D'Arthur is Sir Thomas Malory's richly evocative and enthralling version of the Arthurian legend. Recounting Arthur's birth, his ascendancy to the throne after claiming Excalibur, his ill-fated marriage to Guinevere, the treachery of Morgan le Fay and the exploits of the Knights of the Round Table, it magically weaves together adventure, battle, love and enchantment. *Le Morte D'Arthur* looks back to an idealized medieval world and is full of wistful, elegiac regret for a vanished age of chivalry. Edited and published by William Caxton in 1485, Malory's prose romance drew on French and English verse sources to give an epic unity to the Arthur myth, and remains the most magnificent re-telling of the story in English.

The text of this edition is based on Caxton's original printed edition, with modernized spelling and punctuation. John Lawlor's introduction discusses the figure of Arthur, the life and career of Malory and his unique prose style. This volume also contains notes and a glossary.

Edited by Janet Cowen with an introduction by John Lawlor

THE STORY OF PENGUIN CLASSICS

Before 1946 ... 'Classics' are mainly the domain of academics and students; readable editions for everyone else are almost unheard of. This all changes when a little-known classicist, E. V. Rieu, presents Penguin founder Allen Lane with the translation of Homer's *Odyssey* that he has been working on in his spare time.

1946 Penguin Classics debuts with *The Odyssey*, which promptly sells three million copies. Suddenly, classics are no longer for the privileged few.

1950s Rieu, now series editor, turns to professional writers for the best modern, readable translations, including Dorothy L. Sayers's *Inferno* and Robert Graves's unexpurgated *Twelve Caesars*.

1960s The Classics are given the distinctive black covers that have remained a constant throughout the life of the series. Rieu retires in 1964, hailing the Penguin Classics list as 'the greatest educative force of the twentieth century.'

1970s A new generation of translators swells the Penguin Classics ranks, introducing readers of English to classics of world literature from more than twenty languages. The list grows to encompass more history, philosophy, science, religion and politics.

1980s The Penguin American Library launches with titles such as *Uncle Tom's Cabin*, and joins forces with Penguin Classics to provide the most comprehensive library of world literature available from any paperback publisher.

1990s The launch of Penguin Audiobooks brings the classics to a listening audience for the first time, and in 1999 the worldwide launch of the Penguin Classics website extends their reach to the global online community.

The 21st Century Penguin Classics are completely redesigned for the first time in nearly twenty years. This world-famous series now consists of more than 1300 titles, making the widest range of the best books ever written available to millions – and constantly redefining what makes a 'classic'.

The Odyssey continues ...

The best books ever written

PENGUIN CLASSICS

SINCE 1946

Find out more at www.penguinclassics.com